ESSAYS

BY

ELIZABETH BARRETT BROWNING.

ESSAYS

ON THE

GREEK CHRISTIAN POETS

AND THE

ENGLISH POETS

BY

ELIZABETH BARRETT BROWNING

NEW YORK:
PUBLISHED BY JAMES MILLER,
(SUCCESSOR TO C. S. FRANCIS & CO.,)
522 BROADWAY.
1864.

NOTE BY THE AMERICAN PUBLISHER.

THIS little book of prose, added to MRS. BROWNING's previous books of verse, completes the publication of her works. These stand now in five volumes, uniform with the present, including a MEMORIAL by Theodore Tilton.

JAMES MILLER.

PREFACE TO THE LONDON EDITION.

The following pieces, first printed in 1842 by the "Athonœum," are now reprinted with the liberal permission of that journal.

It was intended by its writer, that the account of the Greek Christian Poets should receive corrections, or certainly additions: a project which new objects of interest came to delay. The glancing series of notes upon the English Poets seems suggested by, as well as consequent upon, the account; unless it arose from the publication of Wordsworth's "Poems of early and late years, including The Borderers,"—in the form of a review of which, the latter part of the paper originally appeared: the former was occasioned by "The Book of the Poets," a compilation of the day.

Both performances, laid away long ago, and only lately unfolded for the first time, were perhaps almost forgotten by their author; but on the whole, in all likelihood, some way or other reproduction was desired: and this is effected accordingly.

A name, which occurs unworthily enough toward the close, should be withdrawn were it found possible: its presence may be pardoned, as serving at least to mark more dates than one.

LONDON, *February*, 1863.

SOME ACCOUNT

OF THE

GREEK CHRISTIAN POETS.

The Greek language was a strong intellectual life, stronger than any similar one which has lived in the breath of "articulately speaking men," and survived it. No other language has lived so long and died so hard,—pang by pang, each with a dolphin color—yielding reluctantly to that doom of death and silence which must come at last to the speaker and the speech. Wonderful it is to look back fathoms down the great Past, thousands of years away—where whole generations lie unmade to dust—where the sounding of their trumpets, and the rushing of their scythed chariots, and that great shout which brought down the birds stone dead from beside the sun, are more silent than the dog breathing at our feet, or the fly's paces on our window-pane; and yet, from the heart of which silence, to feel *words* rise up like a smoke—words of men, even words of women, uttered at first, perhaps, in "excellent low voices," but audible and distinct to our times, through "the dreadful pother" of life and death, the hissing of the steam-engine and the cracking of the cerement! It is wonderful to look back and listen. Blind Homer spoke this Greek after blind Demodocus, with a quenchless light about his brows, which he felt through his blindness. Pindar rolled his chariots in it, prolonging the clamor of the games. Sappho's heart beat through it, and heaved up the world's. Æschylus strained it to the stature of his high thoughts. Plato crowned it with his divine peradventures. Aristophanes made it drunk with the wine of his fantastic merriment. The later Platonists wove their souls away in it, out of sight of other souls. The first Christians heard in it God's new revelation, and confessed their Christ in it from the suppliant's knee, and presently from the bishop's throne. To all times, and their transitions, the language lent itself. Through the long summer of above two thousand years, from the grasshopper Homer sang of, to that grasshopper of Manuel Phile, which might indeed have been "a burden," we can in nowise mistake the chirping of the bloodless, deathless, wondrous creature. It chirps on in Greek still. At the close of that long summer, though Greece lay withered to her root, her academic groves and philosophic gardens all leafless and bare, still from the depth of the desolation rose up the voice—

> O cuckoo, shall I call thee bird,
> Or but a wandering voice?

which did not grow hoarse, like other cuckoos, but sang not unsweetly, if more faintly than before. Strangely vital was this Greek language—

> Some straggling spirits were behind, to be
> Laid out with most thrift on its memory.

It seemed as if nature could not part with so lovely a tune—as if she felt it ringing on still in her head—or as if she hummed it to herself, as the watchman used to do, with "night wandering round" him, when he watched wearily on the palace roof of the doomed house of Atreus.

But, although it is impossible to touch with a thought the last estate of Greek poetical literature without the wonder occurring of its being still Greek, still poetry,—though we are startled by the phenomenon of life-like sounds coming up from the ashes of a mighty people—at the aspect of an Alcestis returned from the dead, *veiled*, but identical,—we are forced to admit, after the first pause of admiration, that a change has passed upon the great thing we recognize, a change proportionate to the greatness, and involving a caducity. Therefore, in adventuring some imperfect account of the Greek ecclesiastical poets, it is right to premise it with the full and frank admission, that they are not accomplished poets,—that they do not, in fact, reach, with their highest lifted hand, the lowest foot of those whom the world has honored as Greek poets, but who have honored the world more by their poetry. The instrument of the Greek tongue was, at the Christian era, an antique instrument, somewhat worn, somewhat stiff in the playing, somewhat deficient in notes which it had once, somewhat feeble and uncertain in such as it retained. The subtlety of the ancient music, the variety of its cadences, the intersections of sweetness in the rise and fall of melodies, rounded and contained in the unity of its harmony, are as utterly lost to this later period as the digamma was to an earlier one. We must not seek for them; we shall not find them; their place knows them no more. Not only was there a lack in the instrument,—there was also a deficiency in the players. Thrown aside, after the old flute-story, by a goddess, it was taken up by a mortal hand—by the hand of men gifted and noble in their generation, but belonging to it intellectually, even by their gifts and their nobleness. Another immortal, a true genius, might, nay, would, have asserted himself, and wrung a poem of almost the ancient force from the infirm instrument. It is easy to fancy and to wish that it had been so—that some martyr or bishop, when bishops were martyrs, and the earth was still warm with the Sacrificial blood, had been called to the utterance of his soul's devotion, with the emphasis of a great poet's power. No one, however, was so called. Of all the names which shall presently be reckoned, and of which it is the object of this sketch to give some account, beseeching its readers to hold several in honorable remembrance, not one can be crowned with a steady hand as a true complete poet's name. Such a crown is a sacred dignity, and, as it should not be touched idly, it must not be used here. A born Warwick could find, here, no head for a crown.

Yet we shall reckon names "for remembrance," and speak of things not ignoble—of meek, heroic Christians, and heavenward faces washed serene by tears—strong knees bending humbly for the very strength's sake—bright intellects burning often to the winds in fantastic shapes, but oftener still with an honest, inward heat, vehement on heart and brain—most eloquent fallible lips that convince us less than they persuade—a divine loquacity of human falsities—poetical souls, that are not souls of poets! Surely not ignoble things! And the reader will perceive at once that the writer's heart is not laid beneath the wheels of a cumbrous ecclesiastical antiquity—that its intent is to love what is lovable, to honor what is honorable, and to kiss both through the dust of centuries, but by no means to recognize a *hierarchy*, whether in the church or in literature.

If, indeed, an opinion on the former relation might be regarded here, it would be well to suggest, that to these "Fathers," as we call them filially, with heads turned away, we owe more reverence for the grayness of their beards than theologic gratitude for the outstretching of their hands. Devoted and disinterested as many among them were, they, themselves, were at most times evidently and consciously surer of their *love*, in a theologic sense, than of their knowledge in any. It is no place for a reference to religious controversy; and if it were, we are about to consider them simply as poets, without trenching on the very wide ground of their prose works and ecclesiastical opinions. Still one passing remark may be admissible, since the fact *is* so remarkable—how any body of Christian men can profess to derive their opinions from "the opinions of the Fathers," when *all* bodies might do so equally. These fatherly opinions are, in truth, multiform, and multitudinous as the fatherly "sublime gray hairs." There is not only a father apiece for every child, but, not to speak it unfilially, a piece of every father for every child. Justin Martyr would, of himself, set up a wilderness of sects, besides "something over" for the future ramifications of each several one. What then should be done with our "Fathers"? Leave them to perish by the time-Ganges, as old men innocent and decrepit, and worthy of no use or honor? Surely not. We may learn of them, if God will let us, *love*, and love is much—we may learn devotedness of them and warm our hearts by theirs; and this, although we rather distrust them as commentators, and utterly refuse them the reverence of our souls, in the capacity of theological oracles.

Their place in literature, which we have to do with to-day, may be found, perhaps, by a like moderation. That place is not, it has been admitted, of the highest; and that it is not of the lowest the proof will presently be attempted. There is a mid-air kingdom of the birds called Nephelococcygia, of which Aristophanes tells us something; and we might stand there a moment so as to measure the local adaptitude, putting up the Promethean umbrella to hide us from the "Gods," if it were not for the "men and columns" lower down. But as it is, the very suggestion, if persisted in, would sink all the ecclesiastical antiquity it is desirable to find favor for, to all eternity, in the estimation of the kindest reader. No! the mid-air kingdom of the birds will not serve the wished-for purpose even illustratively, and by grace of the nightingale. "May the sweet saints pardon us" for wronging them by an approach to such a sense, which, if attained and determined, would have consigned them so certainly to what St. Augustine called—when *he* was moderate too—"*mitissima damnatio*," a very mild species of damnation.

It would be, in fact, a rank injustice to the beauty we are here to recognize, to place these writers in the rank of mediocrities, supposing the harsh sense. They may be called mediocrities as poets among poets, but not so as no poets at all. Some of them may sing before gods and men, and in front of any column, from Trajan's to that projected one in Trafalgar Square, to which is promised the miraculous distinction of making the National Gallery sink lower than we see it now. They may, as a body, sing exultingly, holding the relation of column to gallery, in front of the whole "corpus" of Latin ecclesiastical poetry, and claim the world's ear and the poet's palm. That the modern Latin poets have been more read by scholars, and are better known by reputation to the general reader, is unhappily true: but the truth involves no good reason why it should be so, nor much marvel that it is so. Besides the greater accessibility of Latin literature, the vicissitude of life is extended to posthumous fame, and Time, who is Justice to the poet, is sometimes too busy in pulverizing bones to give the due weight to memories. The modern Latin poets, "elegant,"—which is the critic's word to spend upon them,—elegant as they are occasionally, polished and accurate as they are comparatively, stand cold and lifeless, with statue-eyes, near these good, fervid, faulty Greeks of ours—and we do not care to look again. Our Greeks do, in their degree, claim their ancestral advantage, not the mere advantage of language,—nay, least the advantage of language—a comparative elegance and accuracy of expression being ceded to the Latins—but that higher distinction inherent in brain and breast, of vivid thought and quick sensibility. What if we swamp for a moment the Tertullians and Prudentiuses, and touch, by a permitted anachronism, with one hand, VIDA, with the other, GREGORY NAZIANZEN, what then? What though the Italian poet be smooth as the Italian Canova—working like him out of stone—smooth and cold, disdaining to ruffle his dactyls with the beating of his pulses—what then? Would we change for him our sensitive Gregory, with all his defects in the glorious "scientia metrica"? We would not—perhaps we should not, even if those defects were not attributable, as Mr. Boyd, in the preface to his work on the Fathers, most justly intimates, to the changes incident to a declining language.

It is, too, as religious poets, that we are called upon to estimate these neglected Greeks—as religious poets, of whom the universal church and the world's literature would gladly embrace more names than can be counted to either. For it is strange that, although Wilhelm Meister's uplooking and downlooking aspects, the reverence to things above and things below, the religious all-clasping spirit, be, and must be, in degree and measure, the grand necessity of every true poet's soul,—of religious poets, strictly so called, the earth is very bare. Religious "parcel-poets" we have, indeed, more than enough; writers of hymns, translators of Scripture into prose, or of prose generally into rhymes, of whose heart-devotion a higher faculty were worthy. Also there have been poets, not a few, singing as if earth were still Eden; and poets, many, singing as if in the first hour of exile, when the echo of the curse was louder than the whisper of the promise. But the right "genius of Christianism" has done little up to this moment, even for Chateaubriand.

We want the touch of Christ's hand upon our literature, as it touched other dead things—we want the sense of the saturation of Christ's blood upon the souls of our poets, that it may cry *through* them in answer to the ceaseless wail of the Sphinx of our humanity, expounding agony into renovation. Something of this has been perceived in art when its glory was at the fullest. Something of a yearning after this may be seen among the Greek Christian poets, something which would have been *much* with a stronger faculty. It will not harm us in any case, as lovers of literature and honest judges, if we breathe away, or peradventure *besom* away, the thick dust which lies upon their heavy folios, and besom away, or peradventure *breathe* away, the inward intellectual dust, which must be confessed to lie thickly, too, upon the heavy poems, and make our way softly and meekly into the heart of such hidden beauties (hidden and scattered) as our good luck, or good patience, or, to speak more reverently, the intrinsic goodness of the Fathers of Christian Poetry, shall permit us to discover. May gentle readers favor the endeavor, with "gentle airs," if any! readers not too proud to sleep, were it only for Homer's sake; nor too passionate, at their worst displeasure, to do worse than growl in their sleeves, after the manner of "most delicate monsters." It is not intended to crush this forbearing class with folios, nor even with a folio; only to set down briefly in their sight what shall appear to the writer the characteristics of each poet, and to illustrate the opinion by the translation of a few detached passages, or, in certain possible cases, of short entire poems. And so much has been premised, simply that too much be not expected.

It has the look of an incongruity, to begin an account of the Greek Christian poets with a Jew; and Ezekiel is a Jew in his very name, and a "poet of the Jews" by profession. Moreover he is wrapt in such a mystery of chronology, that nobody can be quite sure of his not having lived before the Christian era—and one whole whisper establishes him as a unit of the famous seventy or seventy-two, under Ptolemy Philadelphus. Let us waive the chronology in favor of the mystery. He is brought out into light by Clemens Alexandrinus; and being associated with Greek poets, and a writer himself of Greek verses, we may receive him in virtue of the *τοτοτοτοτοτοτοτοτοτοτιγξ*, with little fear, in his case, of implying an injustice in that middle bird-locality of Nephelococcygia. The reader must beware of confounding him with the prophet; and the circumstance of the latter's inspiration is sufficiently distinguishing. Our Greek Ezekiel is, indeed, whatever his chronology may be, no *vatis* in the ancient sense. A Greek tragedy (and some fragments of a tragedy are all that we hold of him), by a Jew, and on a Jewish subject, "The Exodus from Egypt," may startle the most serene of us into curiosity—with which curiosity begins and ends the only strong feeling we can bring to bear upon the work; since, if the execution of it is somewhat curious too, there is a gentle collateral dulness which effectually secures us from feverish excitement. Moses prologizes after the worst manner of Euripides (worse than the worse), compendiously relating his adventures among the bulrushes and in Pharaoh's household, concluded by his slaying an Egyptian, *because nobody was looking.* So saith the poet. Then follows an interview between the Israelite and Zipporah, and her companions, wherein he puts to her certain geographical questions, and she (as far as we can make out through fragmentary cracks) rather *brusquely* proposes their mutual marriage: on which subject he does not venture an opinion ; but we find him next confiding his dreams in a family fashion to her father, who considers them satisfactory. Here occurs a broad crack down the tragedy—and we are suddenly called to the revelation from the bush by an extraordinarily ordinary dialogue, between Deity and Moses. It is a surprising specimen of the kind of composition adverted to some lines ago, as the translation of Scripture into prose ; and the sublime simplicity of the scriptural narrative being thus done (away) into Greek for a certain time, the following reciprocation,—to which our old moralites can scarcely do more, or less, than furnish a parallel—prays for an English—exposure. The Divine Being is supposed to address Moses:—

But what is this thou holdest in thine hand?—
Let thy reply be sudden.
Moses. 'Tis my rod—
I chasten with it quadrupeds and men.
Voice from the Bush. Cast it upon the ground—and straight recoil;
For it shall be, to move thy wonderment,
A terrible serpent.
Moses. It is cast. But THOU,
Be gracious to me, Lord. How terrible!
How monstrous! Oh, be pitiful to me!
I shudder to behold it, my limbs shake.

The reader is already consoled for the destiny which mutilated the tragedy, without requiring the last words of the analysis. Happily characteristic of the "meekest of men," is Moses's naïve admission of the uses of his rod—to beat men and animals withal—of course "when nobody is looking."

CLEMENS ALEXANDRINUS, to whom we owe whatever gratitude is due for our fragmentary Ezekiel, was originally an Athenian philosopher, afterwards a converted Christian, a Presbyter of the church at Alexandria, and preceptor of the famous Origen. Clemens flourished at the close of the second century. As a prose writer—and we have no prose writings of his, except such as were produced subsequently to his conversion—he is learned and various. His "Pedagogue" is a wanderer, to universal intents and purposes; and his "Tapestry," if the "Stromata" may be called so, is embroidered in all cross-stitches of philosophy, with not much scruple as to the shading of colors. In the midst of all is something, ycleped a dithyrambic ode, addressed to the Saviour, composite of fantastic epithets in the mode of the old litanies, and almost as bald of merit as the Jew-Greek drama, though Clemens himself (worthier in worthier places) be the poet. Here is the opening, which is less fanciful than what follows it:—

Curb for wild horses,
Wing for bird-courses
Never yet flown!
Helm, safe for weak ones,
Shepherd, bespeak once,
The young lambs thine own.
Rouse up the youth,
Shepherd and feeder,

So let them bless thee,
Praise and confess thee,—
Pure words on pure mouth,—
Christ, the child-leader!
Oh, the saints' Lord,
All-dominant word!
Holding, by Christdom,
God's highest wisdom!
Column in place
When sorrows seize us,—
Endless in grace
Unto man's race,
Saving one, Jesus!
Pastor and ploughman,
Helm, curb, together,—
Pinion that now can
(Heavenly of feather)
Raise and release us!
Fisher who catcheth
Those whom he watcheth . . .

It goes on; but we need not do so. "By the pricking of our thumbs," we know that the reader has had enough of it.

Passing rapidly into the fourth century, we would offer our earliest homage to Gregory Nazianzen,

"That name must ever be to us a friend."

when the two APOLINARII cross our path and intercept the "all hail." Apolinarius the grammarian, formerly of Alexandria, held the office of presbyter in the church of Laodicæa, and his son, Apolinarius, an accomplished rhetorician, that of *reader*, an ancient ecclesiastical office, in the same church. This younger Apolinarius was a man of indomitable energies and most practical inferences; and when the edict of Julian forbade to the Christians the study of Grecian letters, he, assisted perhaps by his father's hope and hand, stood strong in the gap, not in the attitude of supplication, not with the gesture of consolation, but in power and sufficiency to fill up the void, and baffle the tyrant. Both father and son were in the work, by some testimony; the younger Apolinarius standing out, by all, as the chief worker, and only one in any extensive sense. "Does Julian deny us Homer?" said the brave man in his armed soul—"I am Homer!" and straightway he turned the whole Biblical history, down to Saul's accession, into Homeric hexameters,—dividing the work, so as to clench the identity of first and second Homers, into twenty-four books, each superscribed by a letter of the alphabet, and the whole acceptable, according to the expression of Sozomen, *αντι της 'Ομηρου ποιησεως*, in the place of Homer's poetry. "Does Julian deny us Euripides?" said Apolinarius again—"I am Euripides!" and up he sprang,—as good a Euripides (who can doubt it?) as he ever was a Homer. "Does Julian forbid us Menander?—Pindar?—Plato?—I am Menander!—I am Pindar!—I am Plato!" And comedies, lyrics, philosophics, flowed fast at the word; and the gospels and epistles adapted themselves naturally to the rules of Socratic disputation. A brave man, forsooth, was our Apolinarius of Laodicæa, and literally a man of men—for, observe, says Sozomen, with a venerable innocence, at which the gravest may smile gravely—as at a doublet worn awry at the Council of Nice,—that the old authors did each man his own work, whereas this Apolinarius did every man's work in addition to his own—and so admirably,—intimates the ecclesiastical critic,—that if it were not for the common prejudice in favor of antiquity, no ancient could be missed in the all-comprehensive representativeness of the Laodicæan writer. So excellent was his ability, to "outbrave the stars in several kinds of light," besides the Cæsar! Whether Julian, naturally mortified to witness this germination of illustrious heads under the very iron of his searing, vowed vengeance against the Hydra-spirit, by the sacred memory of the animation of his own beard, we do not exactly know. To embitter the wrong, Apolinarius sent him a treatise upon truth—a confutation of the pagan doctrine, apart from the scriptural argument,—the Emperor's notice of which is both worthy of his Cæsarship and a good model-notice for all sorts of critical dignities. *Ανεγνων εγνων κατεγνων*, is the Greek of it; so that, turning from the letter to catch something of the point, we may write it down—"I have perused, I have mused, I have abused": which provoked as imperious a retort—"Thou mayst have perused, but thou hast not mused; for hadst thou mused, thou wouldst not have abused." Brave Laodicæan!

Apolinarius's laudable *double* of Greek literature has perished, the reader will be concerned to hear, from the face of the earth, being, like other *lusus*, or marvels, or monsters, brief of days. One only tragedy remains, with which the memory of Gregory Nazianzen has been right tragically affronted, and which Gregory,—*ει τις αισθησις*, as he said of Constantine,—would cast off with the scorn and anger befitting an Apolinarian heresy. For Apolinarius, besides being an epoist, dramatist, lyrist, philosopher, and rhetorician, was, we are sorry to add, in the eternal bustle of his soul, a heretic,—possibly for the advantage of something additional to do. He not only intruded into the churches hymns which were not authorized, being his own composition—so that reverend brows grew dark to hear women with musical voices sing them softly to the turning of their distaff,—but he fell into the heresy of denying a human soul to the perfect MAN, and of leaving the Divinity in bare combination with the Adamic dust. No wonder that a head so beset with many thoughts and individualities should at last turn round!—that eyes rolling in fifty fine phrensies of twenty-five fine poets should at last turn blind!—that a determination to rival all geniuses should be followed by a disposition more baleful in its exercise, to understand "all mysteries"! Nothing can be plainer than the step after step, whereby, through excess of vain-glory and morbid mental activity, Apolinarius, the vice-poet of Greece, subsided into Apolinarius the chief heretic of Christendom.

To go back sighingly to the tragedy, where we shall have to sigh again—the only tragedy left to us of all the tragic works of Apolinarius (but we do not sigh for *that!*)—let no voice evermore attribute it to Gregory Nazianzen. How could Mr. Alford do so, however hesitatingly, in his "Chapters," attaching to it, without the hesitation, a charge upon the writer, whether Gregory or another man, that *he* whoever he was, had of his own free will and choice, destroyed the old Greek originals out of which his tragedy was constructed, and left it a monument of their sacrifice as of the blood on his barbarian hand? The charge passes, not only before a breath, but before its own breath. The tragedy is, in fact, a specimen of *centoism*, which is the adaptation of the phraseology of one work to the construction of another; and we have only to glance at it to perceive the Medæa of Euripides, dislocated into the CHRISTUS PATIENS. Instead of the ancient opening—

Oh, would ship Argo had not sailed away
To Cholchos by the rough Symplegades!
Nor ever had been felled in Pelion's grove
The pine, hewn for her side! . . . .
So she, my queen
Medæa, had not touched this fatal shore
Soul-struck by love of Jason!

Apolinarius opens it thus—

Oh, would the serpent had not glode along
To Eden's garden-land,—nor ever had
The crafty dragon planted in that grove
A slimy snare! So she, rib-born of man,
The wretched misled mother of our race,
Had dared not to dare on beyond worst daring,
Soul-struck by love of—apples!

"Let us alone for keeping our countenance" —and at any rate we are bound to ask gravely of Mr. Alford, *is the Medœa destroyed?*—and if not, did the author of the "Christus Patiens" destroy his originals? and if not, may we not say of Mr. Alford's charge against that author, "Oh, would he had not made it!" So far from Apolinarius being guilty of destroying his originals, it was his reverence for them which struggled with the edict of the persecutor, and accomplished this dramatic adventure;—and this adventure, the only remaining specimen of his adventurousness, may help us to the secret of his wonderful fertility and omnirepresentativeness, which is probably this—that the great majority of his works, tragic, comic, lyric, and philosophic, consisted simply of *centos*. Yet we pray for justice to Apolinarius: we pray for honor to his motives and energies. Without pausing to inquire whether it had been better and wiser to let poetry and literature depart at once before the tyranny of the edict, than to drag them back by the hair into attitudes grotesquely ridiculous—better and wiser for the Greek Christian schools to let them forego altogether the poems of their Euripides, than adapt to the meek sorrows of the tender Virgin-mother, the bold, bad, cruel phrensy of Medæa, in such verses as these—

> She howls out ancient oaths, invokes the faith
> Of pledged right hands, and calls for witness, God!

—we pray straightforwardly for justice and honor to the motives and energies of Apolinarius. "Oh, would that" many lived *now* as appreciative of the influences of poetry on our schools and country, as impatient of their contraction, as self-devoted in the great work of extending them! There remains of his poetical labors, besides the tragedy, a translation of David's Psalms into "heroic verse," which the writer of these remarks has not seen,—and of which those critics, who desire to deal gently with Apolinarius, seem to begin their indulgence by doubting the authenticity.

It is pleasant to turn shortly round, and find ourselves face to face, not with the author of "Christus Patiens," but with one antagonistical both to his poetry and his heresy, GREGORY NAZIANZEN. A noble and tender man was this Gregory, and so tender, because so noble;

a man to lose no cubit of his stature for being looked at steadfastly, or struck at reproachfully. "You may cast me down," he said, "from my bishop's throne, but you cannot banish me from before God's." And bishop as he was, his saintly crown stood higher than his tiara, and his loving martyr-smile, the crown of a nature more benign than his fortune, shone up toward both. Son of the bishop of Nazianzen, and holder of the diocese which was his birthplace, previous to his elevation to the level of the storm in the bishopric of Constantinople, little did he care for bishoprics or high places of any kind,—the desire of his soul being for solitude, quietude, and that silent religion, which should "rather be than seem." But his father's head bent whitely before him, even in the chamber of his brother's death,—and Basil, his beloved friend, the "half of his soul," pressed on him with the weight of love; and Gregory feeling their tears upon his cheeks, did not count his own, but took up the priestly office. Poor Gregory! not merely as a priest, but as a man, he had a sighing life of it. His student days at Athens, where he and Basil read together poems and philosophies, and holier things, or talked low and *misopogonistically* of their fellow-student Julian's bearded boding smile, were his happiest days. He says of himself,

As many stones
Were thrown at *me*, as other men had flowers.

Nor was persecution the worst evil; for friend after friend, beloved after beloved, passed away from before his face, and the voice which charmed them living, spoke brokenly beside their graves,—his funeral orations marked severally the wounds of his heart,—and his genius served, as genius often does, to lay an emphasis on his grief. The passage we shall venture to translate, is rather a cry than a song—

Where are my wingèd words? Dissolved in air.
Where is my flower of youth? All withered. Where
My glory? Vanished. Where the strength I knew
From comely limbs? Disease hath changed it too,
And bent them. Where the riches and the lands?
GOD HATH THEM! Yea, and sinners' snatching hands
Have grudged the rest. Where is my father, mother,
And where my blessed sister, my sweet brother?

Gone to the grave!—There did remain for me
Alone my fatherland, till destiny,
Malignly stirring a black tempest, drove
My foot from that last rest. And now I rove
Estranged and desolate a foreign shore,
And drag my mournful life and age all hoar
Throneless and cityless, and childless save
This father-care for children, which I have,
Living from day to day on wandering feet.
Where shall I cast this body? What will greet
My sorrows with an end? What gentle ground
And hospitable grave will wrap me round?
Who last my dying eyelids stoop to close—
Some saint, the Saviour's friend? or one of those
Who do not know him? The air interpose,
And scatter these words too!

The return upon the first thought is highly pathetic; and there is a restlessness of anguish about the whole passage, which consecrates it with the cross of nature. His happy Athenian associations gave a color, unwashed out by tears, to his mind and works. Half apostolical he was, and half scholastical; and while he mused, on his bishop's throne, upon the mystic tree of twelve fruits, and the shining of the river of life, he carried, as Milton did, with a gentle and not ungraceful distraction, both hands full of green trailing branches from the banks of the Cephissus, nay, from the very plane-tree which Socrates sat under with Phædrus, when they two talked about beauty to the rising and falling of its leaves. As an orator, he was greater, all must feel if some do not think, than his contemporaries; and the "golden mouth" might confess it meekly. Erasmus compares him to Isocrates, but the unlikeness is obvious: Gregory was not excellent at an artful blowing of the pipes. He spoke grandly, as the wind does, in gusts; and, as in a mighty wind, which combines unequal noises, the creaking of trees and rude swinging of doors as well as the sublime sovereign rush along the valleys, we gather the idea, from his eloquence, less of music than of power. Not that he is cold as the wind is—the metaphor goes no further: Gregory cannot be cold, even by disfavor of his antithetic points. He is various in his oratory, full and rapid in allusion, briefly graphic in metaphor, equally sufficient for indignation or pathos, and gifted peradventure with a keener dagger of sarcasm than should hang in a saint's girdle. His orations against Julian have all these characteristics, but they are not poetry, and we must pass down lower, and quite over his beautiful letters, to Gregory, the poet.

He wrote *thirty thousand verses*, among which are several long poems, severally defective in a defect common but not necessary to short occasional poems, and lamentable anywhere, a want of unity and completeness. The excellencies of his prose are transcribed, with whatever faintness, in his poetry—the exaltation, the devotion, the sweetness, the pathos, even to the playing of satirical power about the graver meanings. But although noble thoughts break up the dulness of the groundwork,—although, with the instinct of greater poets, he bares his heart in his poetry, and the heart is worth baring, still monotony of construction without unity of intention is the most wearisome of monotonies, and, except in the case of a few short poems, we find it everywhere in Gregory. The lack of variety is extended to the cadences, and the pauses fall stiffly "*come corpo morto cade.*" Melodious lines we have often: harmonious passages scarcely ever—the music turning heavily on its own axle, as inadequate to living evolution. The poem on his own life ("De Vitâ suâ") is, in many places, interesting and affecting, yet faulty with all these faults. The poem on Celibacy, which state is commended by Gregory as becometh a bishop, has occasionally graphic touches, but is dull enough generally to suit the fairest spinster's view of that melancholy subject. If Hercules could have read it, he must have rested in the middle—from which the reader is entreated to forbear the inference that the poem has not been read through by the writer of the present remarks, seeing that that writer marked the grand concluding moment with a white stone, and laid up the memory of it among the chief triumphs, to say nothing of the fortunate deliverances, *vitæ suæ*. In Gregory's elegiac poems, our ears, at least, are better contented, because the sequence of pentameter to hexameter necessarily excludes the various cadence which they yearn for under other circumstances. His anacreontics are sometimes nobly written, with a certain brave recklessness, as if the thoughts despised the measure—and we select from this class a specimen of his poetry, both because three of his hymns have already appeared in the "Athenæum," and because the anacreontic in question includes to a remarkable extent, the various qualities we have attributed to Gregory, not omitting that play of satirical humor with which he delights to ripple the abundant flow of his thoughts. The writer, though also a translator, feels less misgiving than usual in offering to the reader, in such English as is possible, this spirited and beautiful poem.

SOUL AND BODY.

What wilt thou possess or be?
O my soul, I ask of thee.
What of great or what of small,
Counted precious therewithal?
Be it only rare, and want it,
I am ready, soul, to grant it.
Wilt thou choose to have and hold
Lydian Gyges' charm of old,

So to rule us with a ring,
Turning round the jewelled thing,
Hidden by its face concealed,
And revealed by it's revealed?
Or preferrest Midas' fate—
He who died in golden state,
All things being changed to gold?
Of a golden hunger dying,
Through a surfeit of "would I"-ing!
Wilt have jewels brightly cold,
Or may fertile acres please?
Or the sheep of many a fold,
Camels, oxen, for the wold?
Nay! I will not give thee these!
These to take thou hast not will,
These to give I have not skill;
Since I cast earth's cares abroad,
That day when I turned to God.

Wouldst a throne, a crown sublime,
Bubble blown upon the time?
So thou mayest sit to-morrow
Looking downward in meek sorrow,
Some one walking by thee scorning,
Who adored thee yester morning,
Some malign one? Wilt be bound
Fast in marriage (joy unsound!)

And be turnèd round and round
As the time turns? Wilt thou catch
That sweet sickness? and to match it
Have babies by the hearth, bewildering
And if I tell thee the best children
Are none —what answer?
Wilt thou thunder
Thy rhetorics, move the people under?
Covetest to sell the laws
With no justice in thy cause,
And bear on, or else be borne,
Before tribunals worthy scorn?
Wilt thou shake a javelin rather
Breathing war? or wilt thou gather
Garlands from the wrestler's ring?
Or kill beasts for glorying?
Covetest the city's shout,
And to be in brass struck out?
Cravest thou that shade of dreaming,
Passing air of shifting seeming,
Rushing of a printless arrow,
Clapping echo of a hand?
What to those who understand
Are to-day's enjoyments narrow,
Which to-morrow go again,
Which are shared with evil men,
And of which no man in his dying

Taketh aught for softer lying?
What then wouldst thou, if thy mood
Choose not these? what wilt thou be,
O my soul? a deity?
A God before the face of God,
Standing glorious in His glories,
Choral in His angels' chorus?

Go! upon thy wing arise,
Plumèd by quick energies,
Mount in circles up the skies:
And I will bless thy wingèd passion,
Help with words thine exaltation,
And, like a bird of rapid feather,
Outlaunch thee, Soul, upon the æther

But thou, O fleshly nature, say,
Thou with odors from the clay,
Since thy presence I must have
As a lady with a slave,
What wouldst thou possess or be,
That thy breath may stay with thee
Nay! I owe thee naught beside,
Though thine hands be open wide,
Would a table suit thy wishes.
Fragrant with sweet oils and dishes
Wrought to subtle niceness? where
Stringèd music strokes the air,

And blithe hand-clappings, and the smooth
Fine postures of the tender youth
And virgins wheeling through the dance
With an unveiled countenance,—
Joys for drinkers, who love shame,
And the maddening wine-cup's flame.
Wilt thou such, howe'er decried?
Take them,—and a rope beside!

Nay! this boon I give instead
Unto friend insatiated,—
May some rocky house receive thee,
Self-roofed, to conceal thee chiefly;
Or if labor there must lurk,
Be it by a short day's work!
And for garment, camel's hair,
As the righteous clothèd were,
Clothe thee! or the bestial skin,
Adam's bareness hid within,—
Or some green thing from the way,
Leaf of herb, or branch of vine,
Swelling, purpling as it may,
Fearless to be drunk for wine!
Spread a table there beneath thee,
Which a sweetness shall up-breathe thee,
And which the dearest earth is giving,
Simple present to all living!

When that we have placed thee near it,
We will feed thee with glad spirit.
Wilt thou eat? soft, take the bread,
Oaten cake, if that bested;
Salt will season all aright,
And thine own good appetite,
Which we measure not, nor fetter:
'Tis an uncooked condiment,
Famine's self the only better.
Wilt thou drink? why, here doth bubble
Water from a cup unspent,
Followed by no tipsy trouble,
Pleasure sacred from the grape!
Wilt thou have it in some shape
More like luxury? we are
No grudgers of wine-vinegar!
But if all will not suffice thee,
And thou covetest to draw
In that pitcher with a flaw,
Brimful pleasures heaven denies thee!
Go, and seek out, by that sign,
Other help than this of mine!
For me, I have not leisure so
To warm thee, Sweet, my household foe,
Until, like a serpent frozen,
New-maddened with the heat, thou loosen
Thy rescued fang within mine heart!

Wilt have measureless delights
Of gold-roofed palaces, and sights
From pictured or from sculptured art,
With motion near their life; and splendor
Of bas-relief, with tracery tender,
And varied and contrasted hues?
Wilt thou have, as nobles use,
Broidered robes to flow about thee?
Jewelled fingers? Need we doubt thee?
Gauds for which the wise will flout thee?
I most, who, of all beauty, know
It must be inward, to be so!

And thus I speak to mortals low,
Living for the hour, and o'er
Its shadow, seeing nothing more:
But for those of nobler bearing,
Who live more worthily of wearing
A portion of the heavenly nature—
To low estate of clayey creature,
See, I bring the beggar's meed,
Nutriment beyond the need!
O, beholder of the Lord,
Prove on me the flaming sword!
Be mine husbandman, to nourish
Holy plants, that words may flourish
Of which mine enemy would spoil me,

Using pleasurehood to foil me!
Lead me closer to the tree
Of all life's eternity;
Which, as I have pondered, is
The knowledge of God's greatnesses:
Light of One, and shine of Three,
Unto whom all things that be
Flow and tend!

In such a guise,
Whoever on the earth is wise
Wilt speak unto himself: and who
Such inner converse would eschew,—
We say perforce of that poor wight,
"He lived in vain!" and if *aright*,
It is not the worst word we might.

Amphilochius, bishop of Iconium, was beloved and much appreciated by Gregory, and often mentioned in his writings. Few of the works of Amphilochius are extant; and of these only one is a poem. It is a didactic epistle to Seleucus, "On the Right Direction of his Studies and Life," and has been attributed to Gregory Nazianzen by some writers, upon very inadequate evidence,—that adduced (the similar phraseology which conveys, in this poem and a poem of Gregory's, the catalogue of canonical scriptures), being as easily explained by the imitation of one poet, as by the identity of two. They differ, moreover, upon ground more important than phraseology: Amphilochius appearing to reject, or at least to receive doubtfully, Jude's epistle and the Second of Peter. And there is a harsh force in the whole poem, which does not remind us of our Nazianzen, while it becomes, in the course of dissuading Seleucus from the amusements of the amphitheatre, graphic and effective. We hear, through the description, the grinding of the tigers' teeth, the sympathy of the people with the tigers showing still more savage.

They sit unknowing of these agonies,
Spectators at a show. When a man flies
From a beast's jaw, they groan, as if at least
They missed the ravenous pleasure, like the beast,
And sat there vainly. When, in the next spring,
The victim is attained, and, uttering
The deep roar or quick shriek between the fangs,
Beats on the dust the passion of his pangs,

All pity dieth in that glaring look ;
They clap to see the blood run like a brook ;
They stare with hungry eyes, which tears should fill,
And cheer the beasts on with their soul's good will ;
And wish more victims to their maw, and urge
And lash their fury, as they shared the surge,
Gnashing their teeth, like beasts, on flesh of men.

There is an appalling reality in this picture. The epistle consists of 333 lines, which we mention specifically, because the poet takes advantage of the circumstance to illustrate or enforce an important theological doctrine :—

Three hundred lines, three decads, monads three,
Comprise my poem. *Love the Trinity.*

It would be almost a pain, and quite a regret, to pass from this fourth century, without speaking a word which belongs to it—a word which rises to our lips, a word worthy of honor—Heliodorus. Though a bishop and an imaginative writer, his "Æthiopica" has no claim on our attention, either by right of Christianity or poetry ; and yet we may be pardoned on our part for love's sake, and on account of the false position into which, by negligence of readers or insufficiency of translators, his beautiful romance has fallen, if we praise it heartily and faithfully even here. Our tears praised it long ago, our recollection does so now, and its own pathetic eloquence and picturesque descriptiveness are ripe for any praise. It has, besides, a vivid Arabian Night charm, almost as charming as Scheherazade herself, suggestive of an Arabian Night story drawn out "in many a winding bout," and not merely on the ground of extemporaneous loving and methodical (must we say it?) *lying*. In good sooth—no, not in good sooth, but in evil leasing—every hero and heroine of them all, from Abou Hassan to "the divine Chariclæa," does lie most vehemently and abundantly by gift of nature and choice of author, whether bishop or sultana. "It is," as Pepys observes philosophically of the comparative destruction of gin-shops and churches in the Great Fire of London, "pretty to observe" how they all lie. And although the dearest of story-tellers, our own Chaucer, has told us that "some leasing is, of which there cometh none advauntage to no wight," even that species is used by them magnanimously in its turn, for the bare glory's sake, and without caring for the "advauntage." With equal liberality, but more truth, we write down the bishop of Tricca's romance *charming*, and wish the charm of it (however we may be out of place in naming him among poets), upon any poet who has not yet felt it, and whose eyes, giving honor, may wander over these Remarks. The poor bishop thought as well of his book as we do, perhaps better; for when commanded, under ecclesiastical censure, to burn it or give up his bishopric, he gave up the bishopric. And who blames Heliodorus? He thought well of his romance; he was angry with those who did not; he was weak with the love of it. Let whosoever blames, speak low. Romance-writers are not educated for martyrs, and the exacted martyrdom was very very hard. Think of that English bishop who burnt his hand by an act of volition—only his hand, and which was sure to be burnt afterwards; and how he was praised for it! Heliodorus had to do with a dearer thing—handwriting, not hands. Authors will pardon him, if bishops do not.

NONNUS of Panopolis, the poet of the "Dionysiaca," a work of some twenty-two thousand verses, on some twenty-two thousand subjects shaken together, flourished, as people say of many a dry-rooted soul, at the commencement of the fifth century. He was converted from paganism, but we are sorry to make the melancholy addition, that he never was converted from the "Dionysiaca." The only Christian poem we owe to him—a paraphrase, in hexameters, of the apostle John's gospel—does all that a bald verbosity and an obscure tautology can do or undo, to quench the divinity of that divine narrative. The two well-known words, bearing on their brief vibration the whole passion of a world saved though pain from pain, are thus *traduced*:—

They answered him,
"Come and behold." *Then Jesus himself groaned*
Dropping strange tears from eyes unused to weep.

"Unused to weep!" *Was* it so of the man of sorrows? O obtuse poet! We had translated the opening passage of the Paraphrase, and laid it by for transcription, but are repelled. Enough is said. Nonnus was never converted from the Dionysiaca.

SYNESIUS, of Cyrene, learnt Plato's philosophy so well of Hypatia of Alexandria at the commencement of the fifth century, or rather before, that, to the obvious honor of that fair and learned teacher, he never, as bishop of Ptolemais, could attain to unlearning it. He did not wish to be bishop of Ptolemais; he had divers objections to the throne and the domination. He loved his dogs, he loved his wife; he loved Hypatia and Plato as well as he loved truth; and he loved beyond all things, under the womanly instruction of the former, to have his own way. He was a poet, too; the chief poet, we do not hesitate to record our opinion,—the chief, for true and natural gifts, of all our Greek Christian poets; and it was his choice to pray lyrically between the dew and the cloud rather than preach dogmatically between the doxies. If Gregory shrank from the episcopal office through a meek self-distrust and a yearning for solitude, Synesius repulsed the invitation to it through an impatience of control over heart and life, and for the earnest joy's sake of thinking out his own thought in the hunting-grounds, with no deacon or disciple astuter than his dog to watch the thought in his face, and trace it backward or forward, as the case might be, into something more or less than what was orthodox. Therefore he, a man of many and wandering thoughts, refused the bishopric,—not weepingly, indeed, as Gregory did, nor feigning madness with another of the "nolentes episcopari" of that earnest period,—but with a sturdy enunciation of resolve, more likely to be effectual, of keeping his wife by his side as long as he lived, and of doubting as long as he pleased to doubt upon the resurrection of the body. But Synesius was a man of genius, and of all such true energies as are taken for granted in the name; and the very sullenness of his "nay" being expressive to grave judges of the faithfulness of his "yea and amen," he was considered too noble a man not to be made a bishop of in his own despite, and on his own terms. The fact proves the latitude of discipline, and even of doctrine, permitted to the churches of that age; and it does not appear that the church at Ptolemais suffered any wrong as its result, seeing that Synesius, recovering from the shock militant of his ordination, in the course of which his ecclesiastical friends had "laid hands upon him" in the roughest sense of the word, performed his new duties willingly; was no sporting bishop otherwise than as a "fisher of men"—sent his bow to the dogs, and his dogs to Jericho, that nearest Coventry to Ptolemais, silencing his "stanch hound's authentic voice" as soon as ever any importance became attached to the authenticity of his own. And if, according to the bond, he retained his wife and his Platonisms, we may honor him by the inference, that he did so for conscience' sake still more than love's, since the love was inoperative in other matters. For spiritual fervor and exaltation, he has honor among men and angels; and however intent upon spiritualizing away the most glorified material body from "the heaven of his invention," he held fast and earnestly, as any body's clenched hand could a horn of the altar, the Homoousion doctrine of the Christian heaven, and other chief doctrines emphasizing the divine sacrifice. But this poet has a higher place among poets than this bishop among bishops; the highest, we must repeat our conviction, of all yet named or to be named by us as "Greek Christian poets." Little, indeed, of his poetry has reached us, but this little is great in a nobler sense than of quantity; and when of his odes, Anacreontic, for the most part, we cannot say praisefully that "they smell of Anacreon," it is because their fragrance is holier and more abiding; it is because the human soul burning in the censer, effaces from our spiritual perceptions the attar of a thousand rose-trees whose roots are in Teos. These odes have, in fact, a wonderful rapture and ecstasy. And if we find in them the phraseology of Plato or Plotinus, for he leant lovingly to the latter Platonists,—nay, if we find in them oblique references to the outworn mythology of paganism, even so have we beheld the mixed multitude of unconnected motes wheeling, rising in a great sunshine, as the sunshine were a motive energy,—and even so the burning, adoring poet-spirit sweeps upward the motes of world-fancies (as if, being in the world, their tendency was Godward) upward in a strong stream of sunny light, while she rushes into the presence of "The Alone." We say the *spirit* significantly in speaking of this poet's aspiration. His is an ecstasy of abstract intellect, of pure spirit, cold though impetuous; the heart does not beat in it, nor is the human voice heard; the poet is true to the heresy of the ecclesiastic, and there is no resurrection of the body. We shall attempt a translation of the ninth ode, closer if less graceful and polished than Mr. Boyd's, helping our hand to courage by the persuasion that the genius of its poetry must look through the thickest blanket of our dark.

Well-beloved and glory-laden,
Born of Solyma's pure maiden!
I would hymn Thee, blessed Warden,
Driving from Thy Father's garden
Blinking serpent's crafty lust,

With his bruised head in the dust!
Down Thou camest, low as earth,
Bound to those of mortal birth;
Down Thou camest, low as hell,
Where shepherd-Death did tend and keep
A thousand nations like to sheep,
While weak with age old Hades fell
Shivering through his dark to view Thee.
And the Dog did backward yell
With jaws all gory to let through Thee!
So, redeeming from their pain
Choirs of disembodied ones,
Thou didst lead whom Thou didst gather,
Upward in ascent again,
With a great hymn to the Father
Upward to the pure white thrones!
King, the demon tribes of air
Shuddered back to feel Thee there!
And the holy stars stood breathless,
Trembling in their chorus deathless;
A low laughter fillèd æther—
Harmony's most subtle sire
From the seven strings of his lyre,
Stroked a measured music hither—
Io pæan! victory!
Smiled the star of morning—he
Who smileth to foreshow the day!

Smilèd Hesperus the golden,
Who smileth soft for Venus gay!
While that hornèd glory holden
Brimful from the fount of fire,
The white moon, was leading higher
In a gentle pastoral wise
All the nightly deities!
Yea, and Titan threw abroad
The far shining of his hair
'Neath Thy footsteps holy-fair,
Owning Thee the Son of God;
The Mind artificer of all,
And his own fire's original!

And Thou upon Thy wing of will
Mounting,—Thy God-foot up till
The neck of the blue firmament,—
Soaring, didst alight content
Where the spirit-spheres were singing,
And the fount of good was springing,
In the silent heaven!
Where Time is not with his tide
Ever running, never weary,
Drawing earth-born things aside
Against the rocks; nor yet are given
The plagues death-bold that ride the dreary
Tost matter-depths. Eternity

Assumes the places which they yield!
Not aged, howsoe'er she held
Her crown from everlastingly—
At once of youth, at once of eld,
While in that mansion which is hers,
To God and gods she ministers!

How the poet rises in his "singing clothes" embroidered all over with the mythos and the philosophy! Yet his eye is to the Throne: and we must not call him half a heathen by reason of a Platonic idiosyncrasy, seeing that the esoteric of the most suspicious turnings of his phraseology, is "Glory to the true God." For another ode, Paris should be here to choose it—we are puzzled among the beautiful. Here is one with a thought in it from Gregory's prose, which belongs to Synesius by right of conquest:—

O my deathless, O my blessed,
Maid-born, glorious son confessed,
O my Christ of Solyma!
I who earliest learnt to play
This measure for Thee, fain would bring
Its new sweet tune to citern-string—
Be propitious, O my King!

Take this music which is mine
Anthemed from the songs divine!

We will sing thee deathless One,
God himself and God's great Son—
Of sire of endless generations,
Son of manifold creations!
Nature mutually endued,
Wisdom in infinitude!
God, before the angels burning—
Corpse, among the mortals mourning!
What time Thou wast pourèd mild
From an earthy vase defiled,
Magi with fair arts besprent,
At Thy new star's orient,
Trembled inly, wondered wild,
Questioned with their thoughts abroad—
"What then is the new-born child?
Who the hidden God?
God, or corpse, or king?
Bring your gifts, oh, hither bring
Myrrh for rite—for tribute, gold—
Frankincense for sacrifice!
God! Thine incense take and hold!
King! I bring thee gold of price!
Myrrh with tomb will harmonize!"

For Thou, entombed, hast purified

Earthly ground and rolling tide
And the path of demon nations,
And the free air's fluctuations,
And the depth below the deep!
Thou God, helper of the dead,
Low as Hades didst Thou tread!
Thou King, gracious aspect keep,
Take this music which is mine,
Anthemed from the songs divine.

Eudocia—in the twenty-first year of the fifth century—wife of Theodosius, and empress of the world, thought good to extend her sceptre—

(Hac claritate gemina
O gloriosa fœmina!)

over Homer's poems, and cento-ize them into an epic on the Saviour's life. She was the third fair woman accused of sacrificing the world for an apple, having moved her husband to wrath, by giving away his imperial gift of a large one to her own philosophic friend Paulinus; and being unhappily more learned than her two predecessors in the sin, in the course of her exile to Jerusalem, she took ghostly comfort, by separating Homer's *ειδωλον* from his *φρενες*.

There she sat among the ruins of the holy city, addressing herself most unholily, with whatever good intentions and delicate fingers, to pulling Homer's gold to pieces bit by bit, even as the ladies of France devoted what remained to them of virtuous energy "pour parfiler" under the benignant gaze of Louis Quinze. She, too, who had no right of the purple to literary ineptitude—she, born no empress of Rome, but daughter of Leontius the Athenian, what had she to do with Homer, "parfilant"? Was it not enough for Homer that he was turned once, like her own cast imperial mantle, by Apolinarius into a Jewish epic, but that he must be unpicked again by Eudocia for a Christian epic? The reader, who has heard enough of centos, will not care to hear how she did it. That she did it, was too much; and the deed recoiled. For mark the poetical justice of her destiny; let all readers mark it, and all writers, especially female writers, who may be half as learned, and not half as fair,—that although she wrote many poems, one "On the Persian War," whose title and merit are recorded, not one, except this cento, has survived. The obliterative sponge we hear of in Æschylus, has washed out every verse except this cento's "damned spot." This remains. This is called Eudocia! this stands for the daughter of Leontius, and this only in the world! O fair mischief! she is punished by her hand.

And yet, are we born critics any more than she was born an empress, that we should not have a heart? and is our heart stone, that it should not wax soft within us while the vision is stirred "between our eyelids and our eyes," of this beautiful Athenais, baptized once by Christian waters, and once by human tears, into Eudocia, the imperial mourner?—this learned pupil of a learned father, crowned once by her golden hair, and once by her golden crown, yet praised more for poetry and learning than for beauty and greatness by such grave writers as Socrates and Evagrius, the ecclesiastical historians?—this world's empress, pale with the purple of her palaces, an exile even on the throne from her Athens, and soon twice an exile, from father's grave and husband's bosom? We relent before such a vision. And what, if, relentingly, we declare her innocent of the Homeric cento?—what if we find her "a whipping boy" to take the blame?—what if we write down a certain Proba "improba," and bid her bear it? For Eudocia having been once a mark to slander, may have been so again; and Falconia Proba, having committed centoism upon Virgil, must have been capable of any thing. The Homeric cento has been actually attributed to her by certain critics, with whom we would join in all earnestness our most sour voices, gladly, for Eudocia's sake, who is closely dear to us, and not malignly for Proba's, who was "improba" without our help. So shall we impute evil to only one woman, and she not an Athenian; while our worst wish, even to her, assumes this innoxious shape, that she had used a distaff rather than a stylus, though herself and the yet more "Sleeping Beauty" had owned one horoscope between them! Amen to our wish! A busy distaff and a sound sleep to Proba!

And now, that golden-haired, golden-crowned daughter of Leontius, for whom neither the much learning nor the much sorrow drove Hesperus from her sovran eyes—let her pass on unblenched. Be it said of her, softly as she goes, by all gentle readers—"She is innocent, whether for centos or for apples! She wrote only such Christian Greek poems as Christians and poets might rejoice to read, but which perished with her beauty, as being of one seed with it."

Midway in the sixth century we encounter Paul Silentiarius, called so in virtue of the office held by him in the court of Justinian, and chiefly esteemed for his descriptive poem on the Byzantine church of St. Sophia, which, after the Arian conflagration, was rebuilt gorgeously by the emperor. This church was not dedicated to a female saint, according to the supposition of many persons, but to the second person of the Trinity, the *ἁγια σοφια*—holy wisdom; while the poem being recited in the imperial presence, and the poet's gaze often forgetting to rise higher than the imperial smile, Paul Silentiarius dwelt less on the divine dedication and the spiritual uses of the place, than on the glory of the dedicator and the beauty of the structure. We hesitate, moreover, to grant to his poem the praise which has been freely granted to it by more capable critics, of its power to realize this beauty of structure to the eyes of the reader. It is highly elaborate and artistic; but the elaboration and art appear to us architectural far more than picturesque. There is no sequency, no congruity, no keeping, no light and shade. The description has reference to the working as well as to the work, to the materials as well as to the working. The eyes of the reader are suffered to approach the whole only in analysis, or rather in analysis analyzed. Every part, part by part, is recounted to him excellently well—is brought close till he may touch it with his eyelashes; but when he seeks for the general effect, it is in pieces—there is none of it. Byron shows him more in the passing words—

> I have beheld Sophia's bright roofs swell
> Their glittering mass i' the sun—

than Silentarius in all his poem. Yet the poem has abundant merit in diction and harmony;

and, besides higher noblenesses, the pauses are modulated with an artfulness not commonly attained by these later Greeks, and the ear exults in an unaccustomed rhythmetic pomp which the inward critical sense is inclined to murmur at, as an expletive verbosity.

Whoever looketh with a mortal eye
To heaven's emblazoned forms, not steadfastly
With unreverted neck can bear to measure
That meadow-round of star-apparelled pleasure,
But drops his eyelids to the verdant hill,
Yearning to see the river run at will,
With flowers on each side,—and the ripening corn,
And grove thick set with trees, and flocks at morn
Leaping against the dews,—and olives twined,
And green vine-branches trailingly inclined,—
And the blue calmness skimmed by dripping oar
Along the Golden Horn.
But if he bring
His foot across this threshold, never more
Would he withdraw it; fain, with wandering
Moist eyes, and ever-turning head, to stay,
Since all satiety is driven away
Beyond the noble structure. Such a fane
Of blameless beauty hath our Cæsar raised
By God's perfective grace, and not in vain!

O emperor, these labors we have praised,
Draw down the glorious Christ's perpetual smile:
For thou, the high-peaked Ossa didst not pile
Upon Olympus' head, nor Pelion throw
Upon the neck of Ossa, opening so
The æther to the steps of mortals! no!
Having achieved a work more high than hope,
Thou dost not need these mountains as a slope
Whereby to scale the heaven! Wings take thee thither
From purest piety to highest æther.

The following passage, from the same "Description," is hard to turn into English, through the accumulative riches of the epithets. Greek words atone for their vain-glorious redundancy by their beauty, but we cannot think so of these our own pebbles:—

Who will unclose me Homer's sounding lips,
And sing the marble mead that over-sweeps
The mighty walls and pavements spread around,
Of this tall temple, which the sun has crowned?
The hammer with its iron tooth was loosed
Into Carystus' summit green, and bruised
The Phrygian shoulder of the dædal stone;—
This marble, colored after roses fused
In a white air, and that, with flowers thereon
Both purple and silver, shining tenderly!

And that which in the broad fair Nile sank low
The barges to their edge, the porphyry's glow
Sown thick with little stars! and thou mayst see
The green stone of Laconia glitter free!
And all the Carian hill's deep bosom brings,
Streaked bow-wise, with a livid white and red,—
And all the Lydian chasm keeps coverèd,
A hueless blossom with a ruddier one
Soft mingled! all besides, the Libyan sun
Warms with his golden splendor, till he make
A golden yellow glory for his sake,
Along the roots of the Maurusian height!
And all the Celtic mountains give to sight
From crystal clefts: black marbles dappled fair
With milky distillations here and there!
And all the onyx yields in metal-shine
Of precious greenness!—all that land of thine,
Ætolia, hath on even plains engendered
But not on mountain-tops,—a marble rendered
Here nigh to green, of tints which emeralds use,
Here with a sombre purple in the hues!
Some marbles are like new dropt snow, and some
Alight with blackness!—Beauty's rays have come
So congregate, beneath this holy dome!

And thus the poet takes us away from the church and dashes our senses and admirations down these marble quarries! Yet it is right for us to admit the miracle of a poem made out of stones! and when he spoke of unclosing Homer's lips on such a subject, he was probably thinking of Homer's ships, and meant to intimate that one catalogue was as good for him as another.

John Geometra arose in no propitious orient probably with the seventh century, although the time of his "elevation" appears to be uncertain within a hundred years.

He riseth slowly, as his sullen car
Had all the weights of sleep and death hung on it.

Plato, refusing his divine fellowship to any one who was not a geometrician or who was a poet, might have kissed our Johannes, who was not divine, upon both cheeks, in virtue of his other name and in vice of his verses. He was the author of certain hymns to the Virgin Mary, as accumulative of epithets and admirations as ten of her litanies, inclusive of a pious compliment, which, however geometrically exact in its proportions, sounds strangely.

O health to thee! new living car of the sky
  Afire on the wheels of four virtues at once!
O health to thee! Seat, than the cherubs more high,
  More pure than the seraphs, *more broad than the thrones!*

Toward the close of the last hymn, the exhausted poet empties back something of the ascription into his own lap, by a remarkable "mihi quoque."

O health to me, royal one! if there belong
  Any grace to my singing, that grace is from thee.
O health to me, royal one! if in my song
  Thou hast pleasure, oh, thine is the grace of the glee!

We may mark the time of GEORGE PISIDA, about thirty years deep in the seventh century. He has been confounded with the rhetorical archbishop of Nicomedia, but held the office of scævophylax, only lower than the highest, in the metropolitan church of St. Sophia, and was a poet, singing half in the church and half in the court, and considerably nearer to the feet of the Emperor Heraclius than can please us in any measure. Hoping all things, however, in our poetical charity, we are willing to hope even this,—that the man whom Heraclius carried about with him as a singing-man when he went to fight the Persians, and who sang and recited accordingly, and provided notes of admiration for all the imperial notes of interrogation, and gave his admiring poems the appropriate and suggestive name of *acroases* — auscultations, things intended to be heard,—might nevertheless love Heraclius the fighting-man, not slave-wise or flatter-wise, but man-wise or dog-wise, in good truth, and up to the brim of his praise; and so hoping, we do not dash the praise down as a libation to the infernal task-masters. Still it is an impotent conclusion to a free-hearted poet's musing on the "Six Days' Work," to wish God's creation under the sceptre of his particular friend! It looks as if the particular friend had an ear like Dionysius, and the poet—ah, the poet!—a mark as of a chain upon his brow in the shadow of his court laurel.

We shall not revive the question agitated among his contemporaries, whether Euripides or George Pisida wrote the best iambics; but that our George knew the secret of beauty, and that having noble thoughts, he could utter them nobly, is clear, despite of Heraclius. That he is, besides, unequal; often coldly perplexed when he means to be ingenious, only violent when he seeks to be inspired; that he premeditates ecstasies, and is inclined to the attitudes of the orators; in brief, that he "not only" (and not seldom) "sleeps but *snores*" are facts as true of him as the praise is. His Hexaëmeron, to which we referred as his chief work, is rather a meditation or rhythmetical speech upon the finished creation, than a retrospection of the six days; and also there is more of Plato in it than of Moses. It has many fine things, and whole passages of no ordinary eloquence, though difficult to separate and select.

Whatever eyes seek God to view His Light,
As far as they behold Him close in night!
Whoever searcheth with insatiate balls
Th' abysmal glare, or gazeth on Heaven's walls
Against the fire-disk of the sun, the same
According to the vision he may claim,
Is dazzled from his sense. What soul of flame
Is called sufficient to view onward thus
The way whereby the sun's light came to us?

O distant Presence in fixed motion! Known
To all men, and inscrutable to one:
Perceived—uncomprehended! unexplained
To all the spirits, yet by each attained,
Because its God-sight is Thy work! O Presence,
Whatever holy greatness of Thine essence
Lie virtue-hidden, Thou hast given our eyes
The vision of Thy plastic energies—
Not shown in angels only (those create
All fiery-hearted, in a mystic state
Of bodiless body) but, if order be
Of natures more sublime than they or we,
In highest Heaven, or mediate æther, or
This world now seen, or one that came before,
Or one to come,—quick in Thy purpose,—*there!*
Working in fire and water, earth and air—
In every tuneful star, and tree, and bird—
In all the swimming, creeping life unheard,
In all green herbs, and chief of all, in MAN.

There are other poems of inferior length, "On the Persian War," in three books, or, alas, "auscultations,"—"The Heracliad," again on the Persian war, and in two (of course) auscultations again,—"Against Severus," "On the Vanity of Life," "The War of the Huns," and others. From the "Vanity of Life," which has much beauty and force, we shall take a last specimen :—

Some yearn to rule the state, to sit above,
And touch the cares of hate as near as love;
Some their own reason for tribunal take,
And for all thrones the humblest prayers they make;
Some love the orator's vain-glorious art,—
The wise love silence and the hush of heart,—
Some to ambition's spirit-curse are fain,
That golden apple with a bloody stain;
While some do battle in her face (more rife
Of noble ends) and conquer strife with strife:
And while your groaning tables gladden these,
Satiety's quick chariot to disease,
Hunger the wise man helps, to water, bread,
And light wings to the dreams about his head.

The truth becomes presently obvious, that—

The sage o'er all the world his sceptre waves,
And earth is common ground to thrones and graves.

JOHN DAMASCENUS, to whom we should not give by any private impulse of admiration the title of Chrysorrhoas, accorded to him by his times, lived at Damascus, his native city, early in the eighth century, holding an unsheathed sword of controversy until the point drew down the lightning. He retired before the affront rather than the injury; and in company with his beloved friend and fellow-poet, Cosmas of Jerusalem (whose poetical remains the writer of these remarks has vainly sought the sight of, and therefore can only, as by hearsay, ascribe some value to them), hid the remnant of his life in the monastery of Saba, where Phocas of the twelfth century looked upon the tomb of either poet. John Damascenus wrote several acrostics on the chief festivals of the churches, which are not much better, although very much longer, than acrostics need be. When he writes out of his heart, without looking to the first letters of his verses,—as, indeed, in his Anacreontic his eyes are too dim for iota-hunting,—he is another man, and almost a strong man; for the heart being sufficient to speak, we want no Delphic oracle—"Pan is NOT dead." In our selection from the Anacreontic hymn, the tears seem to trickle audibly; we welcome them as a Castalia, or, rather, "as Siloa's brook," flowing by an oracle more divine than any Grecian one:—

From my lips in their defilement,
From my heart in its beguilement,
From my tongue which speaks not fair,
From my soul stained everywhere,
O my Jesus, take my prayer!

Spurn me not for all it says,
Not for words and not for ways,
Not for shamelessness endued!
Make me brave to speak my mood,
O my Jesus, as I would!
Or teach me, which I rather seek,
What to do and what to speak.

I have sinnèd more than she,
Who learning where to meet with Thee,
And bringing myrrh, the highest-priced,
Anointed bravely, from her knee,
Thy blessed feet accordingly,
My God, my Lord, my Christ!
As Thou saidest not "Depart,"
To that suppliant from her heart,
Scorn me not, O Word, that art
The gentlest one of all words said!
But give Thy feet to me instead,
That tenderly I may them kiss
And clasp them close, and never miss
With over-dropping tears as free

And precious as that myrrh could be,
T' anoint them bravely from my knee!
Wash me with my tears: draw nigh me,
That their salt may purify me.
THOU remit my sins who knowest
All the sinning to the lowest—
Knowest all my wounds, and seest
All the stripes Thyself decreest;
Yea, but knowest all my faith,
Seest all my force to death,
Hearest all my wailings low,
That mine evil should be so!
Nothing hidden but appears
In Thy knowledge, O Divine,
O Creator, Saviour mine—
Not a drop of falling tears,
Not a breath of inward moan,
Not a heart-beat—which is gone!

After this deep pathos of Christianity, we dare not say a word; we dare not even praise it as poetry: our heart is stirred, and not "idly." The only sound which can fitly succeed the cry of the contrite soul, is that of Divine condonation or of angelic rejoicing. Let us who are sorrowful still, be silent too.

Although doubts, as broad as four hundred

years, separate the earliest and latest period talked of as the age of SIMEON METAPHRASTES by those "viri illustrissimi" the classical critics, we may set him down, without much peril to himself or us, at the close of the tenth century, or very early in the eleventh. He is chiefly known for his "Lives of the Saints," which have been lifted up as a mark both for honor and dishonor; which Psellus hints at as a favorite literature of the angels, which Leo Allatius exalts as chafing the temper of the heretics, and respecting which we, in an exemplar serenity, shall straightway accede to one half of the opinion of Bellarmine—that the work speaketh not as things actually happened, but as they might have happened—"*non ut res gestæ fuerant, sed ut geri potuerant.*" *Our* half of this weighty opinion is the first clause—we demur upon "*ut geri potuerant,*"—and we need not go further than the former to win a light of commentary for the term "metaphrases," applied to the saintly biographies in otherwise a doubtful sense, and worn obliquely upon the sleeve of the biographer Metaphrastes, in no doubtful token of his skill in metamorphosing things as they were into things as they might have been. And Simeon having received from Constantinople the honor of his birth within her walls, and returning to her the better honor of the distinctions and usefulness of his life,—so writeth Psellus, his encomiast, with a graceful turn of thought,—expired in an "odor of sanctity" befitting the biographer of all the saints,—breathing out from his breathless remains such an incense of celestial sweetness, that if it had not been for the maladroitness of certain unfragrant persons whose desecration of the next tomb acted instantly as a stopper, the whole earth might at this day be *metaphrased* to our nostrils, as steeped in an attar-gul of Eden or Ede!—we might be dwelling in a phœnix-nest at this day. Through the maladroitness, however, in question, there is lost to us every sweeter influence from the life and death of Simeon Metaphrastes than may result from the lives and deaths of his saints, and from other works of his, whether commentaries, orations, or poems; and we cannot add that the aroma from his writings bears any proportion in value to the fragrance from his sepulchre. Little of his poetry has reached us, and we are satisfied with the limit. There were three Simeons, who did precede our Simeon, as the world knoweth, and whose titles were Stylitæ or Columnarii, because it pleased them in their saintly volition to take the highest place and live out their natural lives supernaturally, each upon the top of a column. Peradventure the columns which our Simeon refused to live upon, conspired against his poetry: peradventure it is on their account that we find ourselves between two alphabetic acrostics, written solemnly by his hand, and take up one wherein every alternate line begins with a letter of the alphabet; its companion in the couplet being left to run behind it, out of livery and sometimes out of breath. Will the public care to look upon such a curiosity? Will our verse writers care to understand what harm may be done by a conspiration of columns—gods and men quite on one side? And will candid readers care to confess at last, that there is an earnestness in the poem, acrostic as it is,—a leaning to beauty's side,—which is above the acrosticism? Let us try:—

Ah, tears upon mine eyelids, sorrow on mine heart,
  I bring Thee soul-repentance, Creator as Thou art!
Bounding joyous actions, deep as arrows go;
  Pleasures self-revolving, issue into woe!
Creatures of our mortal, headlong rush to sin:
  I have seen them; of them—ah me,—I have been!
Duly pitying Spirits, from your spirit-frame,
  Bring your cloud of weeping,—worthy of the same!
Else I would be bolder; if that light of Thine,
  Jesus, quell the evil, let it on me shine!
Fail me truth, is living, less than death forlorn,
  When the sinner readeth—"better be unborn"?
God, I raise toward Thee both eyes of my heart,
  With a sharp cry—"Help me!"—while mine hopes
    depart.
Help me! Death is bitter, all hearts comprehend;
  But I fear beyond it—end beyond the end!
Inwardly behold me, how my soul is black:
  Sympathize in gazing, do not spurn me back!
Knowing that Thy pleasure is not to destroy,
  That Thou fain wouldst save me—this is all my joy.
Lo, the lion, hunting spirits in their deep,
  (Stand beside me!) roareth (help me!) nears to leap!
Mayst Thou help me, Master: Thou art pure alone,

Thou alone art sinless, one Christ on a throne.
Nightly deeds I loved them, hated day's instead;
Hence this soul-involving darkness on mine head.
O Word, who constrainest things estranged and curst,
If Thy hand can save me, that work were the first!
Pensive o'er my sinning, counting all its ways,
Terrors shake me, waiting adequate dismays.
Quenchless glories many, hast Thou—many a rod—
Thou, too, hast Thy measures. Can I bear Thee, God?
Rend away my counting from my soul's decline,
Show me of the portion of those saved of Thine!
Slow drops of my weeping to Thy mercy run:
Let its rivers wash me, by that mercy won!
Tell me what is worthy, in our dreary now,
As the future glory? (madness!) what, as THOU?
Union, oh, vouchsafe me to Thy fold beneath,
Lest the wolf across me gnash his gory teeth!
View me, judge me gently! spare me, Master bland,
Brightly lift Thine eyelids, kindly stretch Thine hand!
Winged and choral angels! 'twixt my spirit lone,
And all deathly visions, interpose your own!
Yea, my Soul, remember death and woe inwrought—
After-death affliction, wringing earth's to naught!
Zone me, Lord, with graces! Be foundations built
Underneath me; save me! as Thou know'st and wilt!

The omission of our X (in any case too sullen a letter to be employed in the service of an acrostic), has permitted us to write line for line with the Greek; and we are able to infer, to the honor of the Greek poet, that, although he did not live upon a column, he was not far below one, in the virtue of self-mortification. We are tempted to accord him some more gracious and serious justice, by breaking away a passage from his "Planctus Mariæ," the lament of Mary on embracing the Lord's body; and giving a moment's insight into a remarkable composition, which, however deprived of its poetical right of measure, is, in fact, nearer to a poem, both in purpose and achievement, than any versified matter we have looked upon from this metaphrastic hand:—

"O uncovered corse, yet Word of the Living One! self-doomed to be uplifted on the cross for the drawing of all men unto Thee,—what member of Thine hath no wound? O my blessed brows, embraced by the thorn-wreath which is pricking at my heart! O beautiful and priestly One, who hadst not where to lay Thine head and rest, and now wilt lay it only in the tomb, resting *there;* sleeping, as Jacob said, a lion's sleep! O cheeks turned to the smiter! O lips, new hive for bees, yet fresh from the sharpness of vinegar and bitterness of gall! O mouth, wherein was no guile, yet betrayed by the traitor's kiss! O hand, creative of man, yet nailed to the cross, and since, stretched out unto Hades, with help for the first transgressor! O feet, once walking on the deep to hallow the waters of nature! O me, my son! . . . Where is Thy chorus of sick ones?—those whom Thou didst cure of their dis eases, and bring back from the dead? Is none here, but only Nicodemus, to draw the nails from those hands and feet?—none here but only Nicodemus, to lift Thee from the cross, heavily, heavily, and lay Thee in these mother-arms which bore Thee long ago, in thy babyhood, and were glad *then?* These hands, which swaddled Thee then, let them bind Thy grave-clothes now. And yet,—O bitter funerals!——O Giver of life from the dead, liest Thou dead before mine eyes? Must *I*, who said 'hush' beside Thy cradle, wail this passion upon Thy grave? *I*, who washed Thee in Thy first bath, must I drop on Thee these hotter tears? I, who raised Thee high in my maternal arms,—but *then* Thou leapedst,—*then* Thou springedst up in Thy child-play!"

It is better to write so than to stand upon a column. And, although the passage does, both generally and specifically, in certain of its ideas, recall the antithetic eloquence of that Gregory Nazianzen before whom this Simeon must be dumb, we have touched his "oration," so called, nearer than our subject could permit us to do any of Gregory's, because the "Planctus" involves an imagined situation, is poetical in its design. Moreover, we must prepare to look downwards; the poets were descending from the gorgeous majesty of the hexameter and the severe simplicity of iambics, down through the mediate "*versus politici*," a loose metre, adapted to the popular ear, to the lowest deep of a "measured prose,"—which has been likened, but which *we* will not liken, to the blank verse of our times. Presently, we may offer an example from Psellus of a prose acrostic—the reader being delighted with the prospect! "A whole silver threepence, mistress."

MICHAEL PSELLUS lived midway in the eleventh century, and appears to have been a man of much aspiration toward the higher places of the earth. A senator of no ordinary influence, preceptor of the emperor Michael previous to that accession, he is supposed to have included in his instructions the advantages of sovereignty, and in his precepts the most subtle means of securing them. We were about to add that his acquirements as a scholar were scarcely less imperial than those of his pupil as a prince: but the expression might have been inappropriate. There are cases not infrequent, not entirely opposite to the present case, and worthy always of all meditation by such intelligent men as affect extensive acquisition,—when acquirements are not ruled by the man, but rule him. Whatever originates from the mind cannot obstruct her individual faculty; nay, whatever she receives inwardly and marks her power over by creating out of it a *tertium quid*, according to the law of the perpetual generation of spiritual verities, is not obstructive but impulsive to the evolution of faculty; but the erudition, whether it be erudition as the world showed it formerly, or miscellaneous literature, as the world shows it now, the accumulated acquirement of whatever character, which remains *extraneous* to the mind, is and must be in the same degree an obstruction and deformity. How many are there from Psellus to Bayle, bound hand and foot intellectually with the rolls of their own papyrus—men whose erudition has grown stronger than their souls! How many whom we would gladly see washed in the clean waters of a little ignorance, and take our own part in their refreshment! Not that knowledge is bad, but that wisdom is better; and that it is better and wiser in the sight of the angels of knowledge to think out one true thought with a thrush's song and a green light for all lexicon (or to think it without the light and without the song—because truth is beautiful, where they are not seen or heard)—than to mummy our benumbed souls with the circumvolutions of twenty thousand books. And so Michael Psellus was a learned man.

We have sought earnestly, yet in vain,—and the fact may account for our ill-humor,—a sight of certain iambics upon vices and virtues, and Tantalus and Sphinx, which are attributed to this writer, and cannot be in the moon after all:—earnestly, yet with no fairer encouragement to our desire than what befalls it from his *poems* "On the Councils," the first of which, and only the first, through the softness of our charities, we bring to confront the reader:—

Know the holy councils, King, to their utmost number,
Such as roused the impious ones from their world-wide slumber!
Seven in all those councils were: Nice the first containing,
When the godly master-soul Constantine was reigning,
What time at Byzantium, hallowed with the hyssop,
In heart and word, Metrophanes presided as archbishop!
It cut away Arius' tongue's maniacal delusion,
Which cut off from the Trinity the blessed Homoousion—
Blasphemed (O miserable man!) the maker of the creature,
And low beneath the Father cast the equal Filial nature.

The prose acrostic, contained in an office written by Psellus to the honor of Simeon, is elaborated on the words "I sing thee who didst write the metaphrases;" every sentence being insulated, and beginning with a charmed letter.

"Say in a dance how we shall go,
Who never could a measure know?"

why, thus—(and yet Psellus, who did *know* every thing, wrote a synopsis of the metres!)—why, thus:

"Inspire me, Word of God, with a rhythmetic chant, for I am borne onward to praise Simeon Metaphrastes and Logothetes, as he is fitly called, the man worthy of admiration!

"Solemnly from the heavenly heights did the Blessed Ghost descend on thee, wise one, and finding thine heart pure, rested there, there verily in the body!"

Surely we need not write any more. But Michael Psellus was a very learned man.

John of Euchaita (or Euchania, or Theodoropolis,—the three names do appear through the twilight to belong to one city) was a bishop, probably contemporary with Psellus—is only a poet now: we turn to see the voice which speaks to us. It is a voice with a soul in it, clear and sweet and living; and we who have walked long in the desert, leap up to its sound as to the dim flowing of a stream, and would take a deep breath by its side both for the weariness which is gone and the repose which is coming. But it is a rarer thing than a stream in the desert: it is a voice in the desert—the only voice of a city. The city may have three names, as we have said, or the three names may more fitly appertain to three cities—scholars knit their brows and wax doubtful as they talk; but a city denuded of its multitudes it surely is, ruined even of its ruins it surely is: no exhalation arises from its tombs, the foxes have lost their way to it, the bittern's cry is as dumb as the vanished population—only the Voice remains. John Mauropus, of Euchaita, Euchania, Theodoropolis—one living man among many dead, as the Arabian tale goes of the city of enchantment—one speechful voice among the silent, sole survivor of the breath which maketh words, effluence of the soul replacing the bittern's cry —speak to us! And thou shalt be to us as a poet; we will salute thee by that high name. For have we not stood face to face with Michael Psellus and him of the metaphrases? Surely as a poet may we salute *thee!*

His poetry has, as if in contrast to the scenery of circumstances in which we find it, or to the fatality of circumstances in which it has *not* been found (and even Mr. Clarke in his learned work upon Sacred Literature, which is, however, incommunicative generally upon sacred poetry, appears unconscious of his being and his bishopric),—his poetry has a character singularly vital, fresh, and serene. There is nothing in it of the rapture of inspiration, little of the operativeness of art—nothing of imagination in a high sense, or of ear-service in any: he is not, he says, of those—

> Who rain hard with redundancies of words,
> And thunder and lighten out of eloquence.

His Greek being opposed to that of the Silentiarii and the Pisidæ by a peculiar simplicity and ease of collocation which the reader feels lightly in a moment, the thoughts move through its transparency with a certain calm nobleness and sweet living earnestness, with holy upturned eyes and human tears beneath the lids, till the reader feels lovingly too. We startle him from his reverie with an octave note on a favorite literary fashion of the living London, drawn from the voice of the lost city; discovering by that sound the first serial illustrator of pictures by poems, in the person of our Johannes. Here is a specimen from an annual of Euchaita, or Euchania, or Theodoropolis—we may say "annual" although the pictures were certainly not in a book, but were probably ornaments of the beautiful temple in the midst of the city, concerning which there is a tradition. Here is a specimen selected for love's sake, because it "illustrates" a portrait of Gregory Nazianzen :—

What meditates thy thoughtful gaze, my father?
To tell me some new truth? Thou canst not so!
For all that mortal hands are weak to gather,
Thy blessed books unfolded long ago.

These are striking verses, upon the Blessed among women, weeping:—

O Lady of the passion, dost thou weep?
What help can we then through our tears survey,
If such as thou a cause for wailing keep?
What help, what hope, for us, sweet Lady, say?
"Good man, it doth befit thine heart to lay
More courage next it, having seen me so.
All other hearts find other balm to-day—
The whole world's consolation is my woe!"

Would any hear what can be said of a Transfiguration before Raffael's:—

Tremble, spectator, at the vision won thee!
Stand afar off, look downward from the height.
Lest Christ too nearly seen should lighten on thee,
And from thy fleshly eyeballs strike the sight,
As Paul fell ruined by that glory white!
Lo, the disciples prostrate, each apart,
Each impotent to bear the lamping light!
And all that Moses and Elias might,
The darkness caught the grace upon her heart
And gave them strength for! *Thou*, if evermore
A God-voice pierce thy dark,—rejoice, adore!

Our poet was as unwilling a bishop as the most sturdy of the "nolentes"; and there are poems written both in depreciation of, and in retrospective regret for, the ordaining dignity, marked by noble and holy beauties which we are unwilling to pass without extraction. Still we are constrained for space, and must come at last to his chief individual characteristic—to the gentle humanities which, strange to say, preponderate in the solitary voice—to the familiar smiles and sighs which go up and down in it to our ear. We will take the poem "To his old house," and see how the house survives by his good help, when the sun shines no more on the golden statue of Constantine:—

Oh, be not angry with me, gentle house,
That I have left thee empty and deserted!
Since thou thyself that evil didst arouse,
In being to thy masters so false-hearted,
In loving none of those who did possess thee,
In minist'ring to no one to an end,
In no one's service caring to confess thee,
But loving still the change of friend for friend,
And sending the last, plague-wise, to the door!
And so, or ere thou canst betray and leave me,
I, a wise lord, dismiss thee, servitor,
And antedate the wrong thou mayst achieve me

Against my will, by what my will allows;
Yet not without some sorrow, gentle house!

For oh, beloved house! what time I render
My last look back on thee I grow more tender!
Pleasant possession, hearth for father's age,
Dear gift of buried hands, sole heritage!
My blood is stirred; and love, that learnt its play
From all sweet customs, moves mine heart thy way!
For thou wast all my nurse and helpful creature,
For thou wast all my tutor and my teacher;
In thee through lengthening toils I struggled deep,
In thee I watched all night without its sleep,
In thee I worked the wearier daytime out,
Exalting truth, or trying by a doubt.
. . . .

And oh, my father's roof! the memory leaves
Such pangs as break mine heart, beloved eaves;
But God's word conquers all! . . . .

He is forced to a strange land, reverting with this benediction to the "dearest house":—

Farewell, farewell, mine own familiar one,
Estranged for evermore from this day's sun,
Fare-thee-well so! Farewell, O second mother,
O nurse and help,—remains there not another!
My bringer-up to some sublimer measure

Of holy childhood and perfected pleasure!
Now other spirits must thou tend and teach,
And minister thy quiet unto each,
For reasoning uses, if they love such use,
But nevermore to me! God keep thee, house,
God keep thee, faithful corner, where I drew
So calm a breath of life! And God keep you,
Kind neighbors! Though I leave you by His grace,
Let no grief bring a shadow to your face;
Because whate'er He willeth to be done
His will makes easy, makes the distant—one,
And soon brings all embraced before His throne!

We pass PHILIP SOLITARIUS, who lived at the close of this eleventh century, even as we have passed one or two besides of his fellow-poets: because they, having hidden themselves beyond the reach of our eyes and the endeavor of our hands, and we being careful to speak by knowledge rather than by testimony, nothing remains to us but this same silent passing—this regretful one, as our care to do better must testify—albeit our fancy will not, by any means, account them, with all their advantages of absence, "the best part of the solemnity."

Early in the twelfth century we are called

to the recognition of THEODORE PRODROMUS, theologian, philosopher, and poet. His poems are unequal, consisting principally of a series of tetrastichs (Greek epigrams for lack of point, French epigrams for lack of poetry) upon the Old and New Testaments, and the Life of Chrysostom,—all nearly as bare of the rags of literary merit as might be expected from the design; and three didactic poems upon Love, Providence, and against Bareus the heretic, into which the poet has cast the recollected life of his soul. The soul deports herself as a soul should, with a vivacity and energy which work outward and upward into eloquence. The sentiments are lofty, the expression free; there is an instinct to a middle and an end. Music we miss, even to the elementary melody: the poet thinks his thoughts, and speaks them; not indeed what all poets, so called, do esteem a necessary effort, and indeed what we should thank him for doing; but he *sings* them in nowise, and they are not of that divine order which are crowned by right of their divinity with an inseparable aureole of sweet sound. His poem upon

Love,—*φιλια* says the Greek word, but friendship does not answer to it,—is a dialogue between the personification and a stranger. It opens thus dramatically, the stranger speaking:

Love! Lady diademed with honor, whence
And whither goest thou? Thy look presents
Tears to the lid, thy mien is vext and low,
Thy locks fall wildly from thy drooping brow
Thy blushes are all pale, thy garb is fit
For mourning in, and shoon and zone are loose!
So changed thou art to sadness every whit,
And all that pomp and purple thou didst use,
That seemly sweet, that new rose on the mouth,
Those fair-smoothed tresses, and that graceful zone,
Bright sandals, and the rest thou haddest on,
Are all departed, gone to naught together!
And now thou walkest mournful in the train
Of mourning women!—where and whence, again?
Love. From earth to God my Father.
Stranger. Dost thou say
That earth of Love is desolated?
Love. Yea!
It so much scorned me.
Stranger. Scorned?
Love. And cast me out
From its door.

Stranger. From its door?
Love. As if without
I had my lot to die!

Love consents to give her confidence to the wondering stranger; whereupon, as they sit in the shadow of a tall pine, she tells a Platonic story of all the good she had done in heaven before the stars, and the angels, and the throned Triad, and of all her subsequent sufferings on the melancholy and ungrateful earth. The poem, which includes much beauty, ends with a quaint sweetness in the troth-plighting of the stranger and the lady. Mayst thou have been faithful to that oath, O Theodore Prodromus! but thou didst swear "too much to be believed—so *much.*"

The poems "On Providence" and "Against Bareus" exceed the "Love," perhaps, in power and eloquence to the full measure of the degree in which they fall short of the interest of the latter's design. Whereupon we dedicate the following selection from the "Providence" to Mr. Carlyle's "gigmen" and all "respectable persons":—

Ah me! what tears mine eyes are welling forth,
To witness in this synagogue of earth
Wise men speak wisely while the scoffers sing,
And rich men folly, for much honoring!
Melitus trifles,—Socrates decrees
Our further knowledge! Death to Socrates,
And long life to Melitus! . . .

. . . .

Chiefdom of evil, gold! blind child of clay,
Gnawing with fixèd tooth earth's heart away!
Go! perish from us! objurgation vain
To soulless nature, powerless to contain
One ill unthrust upon it! Rather perish
That turpitude of crowds, by which they cherish
Bad men for their good fortune, or condemn,
Because of evil fortune, virtuous men!

. . . .

. . . .

Oh, for a trumpet-mouth! an iron tongue
Sufficient for all speech! foundations hung
High on Parnassus' top to bear my feet!
So from that watch-tower, words which shall be meet,
I may out-thunder to the nations near me—
"Ye worshippers of gold, poor rich men, hear me!
Where do ye wander?—for what object stand?
That gold is earth's ye carry in your hand,
And floweth earthward! bad men have its curse

The most profusely! would yourselves be worse
So to be richer?—better in your purse?
Your royal purple—'twas a dog that found it!
Your pearl of price—a sickened oyster owned it!
Your glittering gems are pebbles, dust-astray;
Your palace-pomp was wrought of wood and clay,
Smoothed rock and moulded plinth! earth's clay,
earth's wood,
Earth's common-hearted stones! Is this your mood,
To honor *earth,* to worship *earth,* nor blush?"
What dost thou murmur, savage mouth? Hush, hush!
Thy wrath is vainly breathed. The depth to tread
Of God's deep judgments, was not Paul's, he said.

The "savage mouth" speaks in power, with whatever harshness: and we are tempted to contrast with this vehement utterance another short poem by the same poet, a little quaint withal, but light, soft, almost tuneful,—as written for a "Book of Beauty," and that not of Euchaita! The subject is "LIFE."

Oh, take me, thou mortal,—thy LIFE for thy praiser!
Thou hast met, found, and seized me, and know'st what
my ways are.
Nor leave me for slackness, nor yield me for pleasure,
Nor look up too saintly, nor muse beyond measure!

There 's the veil from my head—see the worst of my
mourning!
There are wheels to my feet—have a dread of their
turning!
There are wings round my waist—I may flatter and
flee thee!
There are yokes on my hands—fear the chains I decree
thee!
Hold *me!* hold a shadow, the wings as they quiver;
Hold *me!* hold a dream, smoke, a track on the river.
Oh, take me, thou mortal,—thy Life for thy praiser,
Thou hast met not and seized not, nor know'st what
my ways are!
Nay, frown not, and shrink not, nor call me an aspen;
There's the veil from my head! I have dropped from
thy clasping!
A fall-back within it I soon may afford thee;
There are wheels to my feet—I may roll back toward
thee!
There are wings round my waist—I may flee back and
clip thee!
There are yokes on my hands—I may soon cease to
whip thee!
Take courage! I rather would hearten than hip thee!

John Tzetza divides the twelfth century with his name, which is not a great one. In addition to an iambic fragment upon education, he has written indefatigably in the metre *politicus*, what must be read, if read at all, with a corresponding energy,—thirteen "chiliads," of "variæ historiæ," so called after Ælian's,—Ælian's without the "honey-tongue,"—very various histories indeed, about crocodiles and flies, and Plato's philosophy and Cleopatra's nails, and Samson and Phidias, and the resurrection from the dead, and the Calydonian boar,—"every thing under the sun" being, in fact, their imperfect epitome. The omission is simply POETRY! there is no apparent consciousness of her entity in the mind of this versifier; no aspiration towards her presence, not so much as a sigh upon her absence. We do not, indeed, become aware, in the whole course of this laborious work, of much unfolding of faculty—take it lower than the poetical; of nothing much beyond an occasional dry, sly, somewhat boorish humor, which being good humor besides, would not be a bad thing were its traces only more extended. But the general level of the work is a dull talkativeness, a prosy adversity, who is no "Daughter of

Jove," and a slumberousness without a dream. We adjudge to our reader the instructive history of the Phœnix.

A phœnix is a single bird and synchronous with nature,
The peacock cannot equal him in beauty or in stature!
In radiance he outshines the gold; the world in wonder
    yieldeth;
His nest he fixeth in the trees, and all of spices buildeth.
And when he dies, a little worm, from out his body
    twining,
Doth generate him back again whene'er the sun is
    shining.
He lives in Ægypt, and he dies in Æthiopia only, as
Asserts Philostratus, who wrote the Life of Apollonius.
And, as the wise Ægyptian scribe, the holy scribe
    Chœremon,
Hath entered on these Institutes, all centre their esteem
    on,
Seven thousand years and six of age, this phœnix of
    the story,
Expireth from the fair Nile side, whereby he had his
    glory!

In the early part of the fourteenth century, Manuel Phile, pricked emulously to the heart by the successful labors of Tzetza, embraced into identity with himself the remaining half of Ælian, and developed in his poetical treatise "On the Properties of Animals," to which Isachimus Camerarius provided a conclusion, the Natural History of that industrious and amusing Greek-Roman. The Natural History is translated into verse, but by no means glorified; and yet the poet of animals, Phile, has carried away far more of the Ælian honey clinging to the edges of his *patera*, than the poet of the Chiliads did ever wot of. What we find in him is not beauty, what we hear in him is not music, but there is an open feeling for the beautiful which stirs at a word, and we have a scarcely confessed contentment in hearkening to those twice-told stories of birds and beasts and fishes, measured out to us in the low monotony of his chanting voice. Our selections shall say nothing of the live grasshopper, called, with the first breath of this paper, an emblem of the vital Greek tongue; because the space left to us closes within our sight, and the science of the age does not thirst to receive, through our hands, the history of grasshoppers, according to Ælian or Phile either.

Everybody knows what Phile tells us here, that grasshoppers live upon morning dew, and cannot sing when it is dry. Everybody knows that the lady grasshopper sings not at all. And if the moral, drawn by Phile from this latter fact, of the advantage of silence in the female sex generally, be true and important, it is also too obvious to exact our enforcement of it. Therefore we pass by the grasshopper, and the nightingale too, for all her fantastic song; and hasten to introduce to European naturalists a Philhellenic species of *heron*, which has escaped the researches of Cuvier, and the peculiarities of which may account to the philosophic reader for that instinct of the "wisdom of our forefathers," which established an English university in approximation with the Fens. It is earnestly to be hoped that the nice ear in question for the Attic dialect, may still be preserved among the herons of Cambridgeshire:—

A Grecian island nourisheth to bless
A race of herons in all nobleness.
If some barbarian bark approach the shore,

They hate, they flee,—no eagle can outsoar!
But if by chance an Attic voice be wist,
They grow softhearted straight, philhellenist;
Press on in earnest flocks along the strand,
And stretch their wings out to the comer's hand.
Perhaps he nears them with a gentle mind,—
They love his love, though foreign to their kind!
For so the island giveth wingèd teachers,
In true love lessons, to all wingless creatures.

He has written, besides, "A Dialogue between Mind and Phile," and other poems; and we cannot part without taking from him a more solemn tone, which may sound as an "Amen" to the good we have said of him. The following address to the Holy Spirit is concentrated in expression:—

O living Spirit, O falling of God-dew,
O Grace which dost console us and renew,
O vital light, O breath of angelhood,
O generous ministration of things good,
Creator of the visible, and best
Upholder of the great unmanifest!
Power infinitely wise, new boon sublime
Of science and of art, constraining might,

In whom I breathe, live, speak, rejoice, and write,—
Be with us in all places, for all time!

"And now," saith the patientest reader of all, "you have done. Now we have watched out the whole night of the world with you, by no better light than these poetical rushlights, and the wicks fail, and the clock of the universal hour is near upon the stroke of the seventeenth century, and you have surely done!" Surely *not*, we answer; for we see a hand which the reader sees not, which beckons us over to Crete, and clasps within its shadowy fingers a roll of hymns Anacreontical, written by MAXIMUS MARGUNIUS! and not for the last of our readers would we lose this last of the Greeks, owing him salutation. Yet the hymns have, for the true Anacreontic fragrance, a musty odor, and we have scant praise for them in our nostrils. Their inspiration is from Gregory Nazianzen, whose "Soul and Body" are renewed in them by a double species of transmigration; and although we kiss the feet of Gregory's high excellencies, we cannot admit any one of them to be a safe conductor of poetical inspiration. And in union with Margunius's plagiaristic tendencies, there is a wearisome lengthiness, harder to bear. He will knit you to the whole length of an "Honi soit qui mal y pense," till you fall asleep to the humming of the stitches, what time you should be reading the "moral." We ourselves once dropped into a "distraction," as the French say,—for nothing could be more different from what the English say, than our serene state of self-abnegation,—at the beginning of a house-building by this Maximus Margenius: when, reading on some hundred lines with our bare bodily eyes, and our soul starting up on a sudden to demand a measure of the progress, behold he was building it still, with a trowel in the same hand; it was not forwarder by a brick. The swallows had time to hatch two nestfuls in a chimney while he finished the chimney-pot! Nevertheless he has moments of earnestness, and they leave beauties in their trace. Let us listen to this extract from his fifth hymn:—

Take me as a hermit lone
With a desert life and moan;
Only Thou anear to mete
Slow or quick my pulse's beat;
Only Thou, the night to chase,
With the sunlight in Thy face!
Pleasure to the eyes may come
From a glory seen afar,
But if life concentre gloom
Scattered by no little star,
Then, how feeble, God, we are!
Nay, whatever bird there be
(Æther by his flying stirred),
He, in this thing, must be free—
And I, Saviour, am Thy bird,
Pricking with an open beak
At the words that Thou dost speak!
Leave a breath upon my wings,
That above these nether things
I may rise to where Thou art,
I may flutter next Thine heart!
For if a light within me burn,
It must be darkness in an urn,
Unless within its crystalline,
That unbeginning light of Thine
Shine!—O Saviour, *let* it shine!

He is the last of our Greeks. The light from

Troy city, with which all Greek glory began, "threw three-times six," said Æschylus, that man with a soul,—beacon after beacon, into the heart of Greece. "Three-times six," too, threw the light from Greece, when her own heart-light had gone out like Troy's, onward along the ridges of time. Three-times six—but what faint beacons are the last!—sometimes only a red brand; sometimes only a small trembling flame; sometimes only a white glimmer as of ashes breathed on by the wind; faint beacons and far! How far! We have watched them along the cloudy tops of the great centuries, through the ages dark but for them,—and now stand looking with eyes of farewell upon the last pale sign on the last mist-bound hill. But it is the sixteenth century. Beyond the ashes on the hill a red light is gathering; above the falling of the dews a great sun is rising: there is a rushing of light and song upward—let it still be UPWARD! Shakespeare is in the world! And the Genius of English Poetry, she who only of all the earth is worthy (Goethe's spirit may hear us say so, and smile), stooping, with a royal gesture, to kiss the dead lips of the Genius of Greece, stands up her successor in the universe, by virtue of that chrism, and in right of her own crown.

The Book of the Poets.

THE BOOK OF THE POETS.

THE voice of the turtle is heard in the land. The green book of the earth is open, and the four winds are turning the leaves: while Nature, chief secretary to the creative Word, sits busy at her inditing of many a lovely poem,—her "Flower and the Leaf" on this side, her "Cuckoo and the Nightingale" on that, her "Paradise of Dainty Devices" in and out among the valleys, her "Polyolbion" away across the hills, her "Britannia's Pastorals" on the home meadows, her sonnets of tufted primroses, her lyrical outgushings of May blossoming, her epical and didactic solemnities of light and shadow, and many an illustrative picture to garnish the universal annual. What book shall we open side by side with Nature's? First, the book of God. "The Book of the Poets" may well come next—even this book, if it deserve indeed the nobility of its name.

But this book, which is not Campbell's Selection from the British Poets, nor Southey's, nor different from either by being better, resembles many others of the nobly named, whether princes or hereditary legislators, in bearing a name too noble for its desert. This book, consisting of short extracts from the books of the poets, beginning with Chaucer, ending with Beattie, and missing sundry by the way,—we call it indefinitely "A book of the poets," and leave it thankful. The extracts from Chaucer are topsy-turvy—one from the Canterbury Tales, prologue thrown in between two from the Knight's Tale; while Gower may blame "his fortune"—

> (And some men hold opinion
> That it is constellation,)

for the dry specimen crumbled off from his man-mountainism. Of Lydgate there is scarcely a page; of Occleve, Hawes, and Skelton—the two last especially interesting in poetical history,—of Sackville, and the whole generation of dramatists, not a word. "The table is not full," and the ringing on it of Phillips's "Splendid Shilling," will not bribe us to endurance. What! place for Pomfret's platitudes, and no place for Shakespeare's divine sonnets? and no place for Jonson's and Fletcher's lyrics? Do lyrics and sonnets perish out of place whenever their poets make tragedies too, quenched by the entity of tragedy? We suggest that Shakespeare has nearly as much claim to place in any possible book of the poets (though also a book of the poetasters) as ever can have John Hughes, who "as a poet, is chiefly known," saith the critical editor, "by his tragedy of the 'Siege of Damascus.'" Let this book therefore accept our boon, and remain a book of the poets, thankfully if not gloriously,—while we, on our own side, may be thankful too, that in the present days of the millennium of Jeremy Bentham, a more literally golden age than the laureates of Saturnus dreamed withal,—any memory of the poets should linger with the booksellers, and "come up this way" with the spring. The thing is good, in that it is at all. Send a little child into a garden, and he will be sure to bring you a nosegay worth having, though the red weed in it should "side the lily," and sundry of the prettiest flowers be held stalk upwards. Flowers are flowers and poets are poets, and "A book of the poets" must be right welcome at every hour of the clock.

For the preliminary essay, which is very moderately well done, we embrace it, with our fingers at least, in taking up the volume. It pleases us better on the solitary point of the devotional poets than Mr. Campbell's beautiful treatise, doing, as it seems to us, more frank justice to the Withers's, the Quarles's and the Crashaws. Otherwise the criticism and philosophy to be found in it are scarcely of the happiest,—although even the first astonishing paragraph which justifies the utility of poetry on the ground of its being an attractive variety of language, a persuasive medium for abstract ideas, (as reasonable were the justification of a seraph's essence deduced from the cloud beneath his foot!)—shall not provoke us back to discontent from the vision of the poets of England, suggested by the title of this "Book," and stretching along gloriously to our survey.

Our poetry has an heroic genealogy. It arose where the sun rises, in the far East. It came out from Arabia, and was tilted on the lance-heads of the Saracens into the heart of Europe, Armorica catching it in rebound from Spain, and England from Armorica. It issued in its first breath from Georgia, wrapt in the gathering-cry of Persian Odin: and passing from the orient of the sun to the antagonistic snows of Iceland, and oversweeping the black pines of Germany and the jutting shores of Scandinavia, and embodying in itself all way-side sounds, even to the rude shouts of the brazen-throated Cimbri,—so modified, multiplied, resonant in a thousand Runic echoes, it rushed abroad like a blast into Britain. In Britain, the Arabic Saracenic Armorican, and the Georgian Gothic Scandinavian mixed sound at last; and the dying suspirations of the Grecian and Latin literatures, the last low stir of the "Gesta Romanorum," with the apocryphal personations of lost authentic voices, breathed up together through the fissures of the rent universe, to help the new intonation and accomplish the cadence. Genius was thrust onward to a new slope of the world. And soon, when simpler minstrels had sat there long enough to tune the ear of the time,—when Layamon and his successors had hummed long enough, like wild bees, upon the lips of our infant poetry predestined to eloquence,—then Robert Langlande, the monk, walking for cloister "by a wode's syde," on the Malvern Hills, took counsel with his holy "Plowman," and sang of other visions than their highest ridge can show. While we write, the woods upon those beautiful hills are obsolete, even as Langlande's verses; scarcely a shrub grows upon the hills! but it is well for the thinkers of England to remember reverently, while, taking thought of her poetry, they stand among the gorse,—that if we may boast now of more honored localities, of Shakespeare's "rocky Avon," and Spenser's "soft-streaming Thames," and Wordsworth's "Rydal Mere," still our first holy poet-ground is there.

But it is in Chaucer we touch the true height,

and look abroad into the kingdoms and glories of our poetical literature,—it is with Chaucer that we begin our "Books of the Poets," our collections and selections, our pride of place and name. And the genius of the poet shares the character of his position: he was made for an early poet, and the metaphors of dawn and spring doubly become him. A morning-star, a lark's exaltation, cannot usher in a glory better. The "cheerful morning face," "the breezy call of incense-breathing morn," you recognize in his countenance and voice: it is a voice full of promise and prophecy. He is the good omen of our poetry, the "good bird," according to the Romans, "the best good angel of the spring," the nightingale, according to his own creed of good luck, heard before the cuckoo.

> Up rose the sunne, and uprose Emilie,

and uprose her poet, the first of a line of kings, conscious of futurity in his smile. He is a king and inherits the earth, and expands his great soul smilingly to embrace his great heritage. Nothing is too high for him to touch with a thought, nothing too low to dower with an affection. As a complete creature cognate of life and death, he cries upon God,—as a sympathetic creature he singles out a daisy from the universe ("si douce est la marguerite"), to lie down by half a summer's day and bless it for fellowship. His senses are open and delicate, like a young child's—his sensibilities capacious of supersensual relations, like an experienced thinker's. Child-like, too, his tears and smiles lie at the edge of his eyes, and he is one proof more among the many, that the deepest pathos and the quickest gayeties hide together in the same nature. He is too wakeful and curious to lose the stirring of a leaf, yet not too wide awake to see visions of green and white ladies between the branches; and a fair house of fame and a noble court of love are built and holden in the winking of his eyelash. And because his imagination is neither too "high fantastical" to refuse proudly the gravitation of the earth, nor too "light of love" to lose it carelessly, he can create as well as dream, and work with clay as well as cloud; and when his men and women stand close by the actual ones, your stop-watch shall reckon no difference in the beating of their hearts. He knew the secret of nature and art, —that truth is beauty,—and saying "I will make 'A Wife of Bath' as well as Emilie, and you shall remember her as long," we do remember her as long. And he sent us a train of pilgrims, each with a distinct individuality apart from the pilgrimage, all the way from Southwark and the Tabard Inn, to Canterbury and Becket's shrine: and their laughter comes never to an end, and their talk goes on with the stars, and all the railroads which may intersect the spoilt earth forever, cannot hush the "tramp, tramp" of their horses' feet.

Controversy is provocative. We cannot help observing, because certain critics observe otherwise, that Chaucer utters as true music as ever came from poet or musician; that some of the sweetest cadences in all our English are extant in his—"swete upon his tongue" in completest modulation. Let "Denham's strength and Waller's sweetness join" the Io pæan of a later age, the "*eurekamen*" of Pope and his generation. Not one of the "Queen Anne's men," measuring out tuneful breath upon their fingers, like ribbons for topknots, did know the art of versification as the old rude Chaucer knew it. Call him rude for the picturesqueness of the epithet; but his verse has, at least, as much regularity in the sense of true art, and more manifestly in proportion to our increasing acquaintance with his dialect and pronunciation, as can be discovered or dreamed in the French school. Critics indeed have set up a system based upon the crushed atoms of first principles, maintaining that poor Chaucer wrote by accent only! Grant to them that he counted no verses on his fingers; grant that he never disciplined his highest thoughts to walk up and down in a paddock—ten paces and a turn; grant that his singing is not after the likeness of their singsong: but there end your admissions. It is our ineffaceable impression, in fact, that the whole theory of accent and quantity held in relation to ancient and modern poetry stands upon a fallacy, totters rather than stands; and that when considered in connection with such old moderns as our

Chaucer, the fallaciousness is especially apparent. Chaucer wrote by quantity, just as Homer did before him, just as Goethe did after him, just as all poets must. Rules differ, principles are identical. All rhythm presupposes quantity. Organ-pipe or harp, the musician plays by time. Greek or English, Chaucer or Pope, the poet sings by time. What is this accent but a stroke, an emphasis, with a successive pause to make complete the time? And what is the difference between this accent and quantity but the difference between a harp-note and an organ-note? otherwise, quantity expressed in different ways? It is as easy for matter to subsist out of space, as music out of time.

Side by side with Chaucer comes Gower, who is ungratefully disregarded too often, because side by side with Chaucer. He who rides in the king's chariot will miss the people's "hic est." Could Gower be considered apart, there might be found signs in him of an independent royalty, however his fate may seem to lie in waiting forever in his brother's ante-chamber, like Napoleon's tame kings. To speak our mind, he has been much undervalued. He is nailed to a comparative degree; and everybody seems to make it a condition of speaking of him, that something be called inferior within him, and something superior out of him. He is laid down flat, as a dark background for "throwing out" Chaucer's lights; he is used as a που στω for leaping up into the empyrean of Chaucer's praise. This is not just nor worthy. His principal poem, the "Confessio Amantis," preceded the "Canterbury Tales," and proves an abundant fancy, a full head and full heart, and neither ineloquent. We do not praise its design,—in which the father-confessor is set up as a story-teller, like the bishop of Tricca "avec l'âme," like the cardinal de Retz, "le moins ecclésiastique du monde,"—while we admit that he tells his stories as if born to the manner of it, and that they are not much the graver, nor, peradventure the holier either, for the circumstance of the confessorship. They are indeed told gracefully and pleasantly enough, and if with no superfluous life and gesture, with an active sense of beauty in some sort, and as flowing a rhythm as may bear comparison with many octosyllabics of our day; Chaucer himself having done more honor to their worth as stories than we can do in our praise, by adopting and crowning several of their number for king's sons within his own palaces. And this recalls that, at the opening of one glorious felony, the Man of Lawe's tale, he has written, a little unlawfully and ungratefully considering the connection, some lines of harsh significance upon poor Gower,—whence has been conjectured by the gray gossips of criticism, a literary jealousy, an unholy enmity, nothing less than a soul-chasm between the contemporary poets. We believe nothing of it; no, nor of the Shakespeare and Jonson feud after it:

> To alle such cursed stories we saie fy

That Chaucer wrote in irritation is clear: that he was angry seriously and lastingly, or beyond the pastime of passion spent in a verse as provoked by a verse, there appears to us no reason for crediting. But our idea of the nature of the irritation will expound itself in our idea of the offence, which is here in Dan Gower's proper words, as extracted from the Ladie Venus's speech in the "Confessio Amantis."

And grete well Chaucer whan ye mete,
As my disciple and poëte!—

. . . . .

Forthy now in his daiës old,
Thou shalt him tellë this message,
That he upon his latter age,
To sette an ende of alle his werke,
As he who is mine ownë clerke,
Do make his testament of love.

We would not slander Chaucer's temper,—we believe, on the contrary, that he had the sweetest temper in the world,—and still it is our conviction, none the weaker, that he was far from being entirely pleased by this "message." We are sure he did not like the message, and not many poets would. His "elvish countenance" might well grow dark, and "his sugred mouth" speak somewhat sourly, in response to such a message. Decidedly, in our own opinion, it was an impertinent message, a provocative message, a most inexcusable and odious message! Waxing hotter ourselves the longer we think of it, there is the more excuse for Chaucer. For, consider, gentle reader! this indecorous message preceded the appearance of the Canterbury Tales, and proceeded from a rival poet in the act of completing his principal work,—its plain significance being "I have done my poem, and you cannot do yours because you are superannuated." And this, while the great poet addressed was looking forward farther than the visible horizon, his eyes dilated with a mighty purpose. And to be counselled by this, to shut them forsooth, and take his crook and dog and place in the valleys like a gray shepherd of the Pyrenees—he, who felt his foot stronger upon the heights! he, with no wrinkle on his forehead deep enough to touch the outermost of inward smooth dreams—he, in the divine youth of his healthy soul, in the quenchless love of his embracing sympathies, in the untired working of his perpetual energies,—to "make an ende of alle his werke" and be old, as if he were not a poet! "Go to, O vain man,"—we do not reckon the age of the poet's soul by the shadow on the dial! Enough that it falls upon his grave.

Occleve and Lydgate both breathed the air of the world while Chaucer breathed it, although surviving him so long as rather to take standing as his successors than contemporaries. Both called him "master" with a faithful reverting tenderness, and, however we are bound to distinguish Lydgate as the higher poet of the two, Occleve's "Alas" may become the other's lips—

> Alas, that thou thine excellent prudence
> In thy bed mortell mightest not bequeath!

For alas! it was not bequeathed. Lydgate's Thebaid, attached by its introduction to the "Canterbury Tales," gives or enforces the occasion for sighing comparisons with the master's picturesque vivacity, while equally in delicacy and intenseness we admit no progress in the disciple. He does, in fact, appear to us so much overrated by the critics, that we are tempted to extend to his poetry his own admission on his monkish dress,—

> I wear a habit of perfection
> Although my life agree not with that same,

and to opine concerning the praise and poetry taken together, that the latter agrees not with that same. An elegant poet—"poeta elegans"—was he called by the courteous Pits,—a questionable compliment in most cases, while the application in the particular one agrees not with that same. An improver of the language he is granted to be by all; and a voluminous writer of respectable faculties, in his position, could scarcely help being so: he has flashes of genius, but they are not prolonged to the point of warming the soul,—can strike a bold note, but fails to hold it on,—attains to moments of power and pathos, but wears, for working days, no habit of perfection.

These are our thoughts of Lydgate; and yet when he ceased his singing, none sang better; there was silence in the land. In Scotland, indeed, poet-tongues were not all mute; the air across the borders "gave delight and hurt not." Here in the South it was otherwise: and unless we embrace in our desolation such *poems* as the rhyming chronicles of Harding and Fabian, we must hearken for music to the clashing of "Bilboa blades," and be content that the wars of the red and white roses should silence the warbling of the nightingales. That figure dropped to our pen's point, and the reader may accept it as a figure—as no more. To illustrate by figures the times and the seasons of poetical manifestation and decay, is at once easier and more reasonable than to attempt to account for them by causes. We do not believe that poets multiply in peace-time like sheep and sheaves, nor that they fly, like partridges, at the first beating of the drum; and we do believe, having a previous faith in the pneumatic character of their gift, that the period of its bestowment is not subject to the calculations of our philosophy. Let, therefore, the long silence from Chaucer and his disciples down to the sixteenth century, be left standing as a fact undisturbed by any good reasons for its existence, or by any other company than some harmless metaphor—harmless and ineffectual as a glow-worm's glitter at the foot of a colossal statue of Harpocrates. Call it, if you please, as Warton does, a "nipping frost succeeding a premature spring;" or call it, because we would not think our Chaucer premature, or the silence cruel—the trance of English Poetry: her breath, once emitted creatively, indrawn and retained,—herself sinking into deep sleep, like the mother of Apollonius before the glory of a vision, to awaken, to leap up (εξεθορε says Philostratus, the narrator) in a flowery meadow, at the clapping of the white wings of a chorus of encircling swans. We shall endeavor to realize this awaking.

Is Hawes a swan? a black (letter) swan? Certain voices will "say nay, say nay;" and already, and without our provocation, he seems to us unjustly depreciated. Warton was called "the indulgent historian of our poetry," for being so kind as to discover "one fine line" in in him! What name must the over-kind have, in whose susceptible memories whole passages stand up erect, claiming the epithet or the like of the epithet,—and that, less as the largess of the indulgent than the debt of the just? Yet Langlande's "Piers Plowman," and Chaucer's "House of Fame," and Lydgate's "Temple of Glasse," and the "Pastyme of Plesure," by Stephen Hawes, are the four columnar marbles, the four allegorical poems, on whose foundation is exalted into light the great allegorical poem of the world, Spenser's "Faery Queen." There was a force of suggestion which preceded Sackville's, and Hawes uttered it. His work is very grave for a pastime, being a course of instruction upon the seven sciences, the trivium and quadrivium of the schools; whereby Grand Amour, scholar and hero, wooing and winning Belle Pucelle, marries her according to the "*lex ecclesiæ*," is happy "all the rest of his life" by the *lex* of all matrimonial romances,—and at leisure and in old age, dies by the *lex naturæ*. He tells his own story quite to an end, including the particulars of his funeral and epitaph; and is considerate enough to leave the reader in full assurance of his posthumous reputation. And now let those who smile at the design dismiss their levity before the poet's utterance:—

O mortall folke you may beholde and see
Howe I lye here, sometime a mighty knight.
The ende of joye and all prosperitie
Is death at last thorough his course and might.
After the day there cometh the dark night,
For though the day appear ever so long,
At last the bell ringeth to even song.

—it "ringeth" in our ear with a soft and solemn music to which the soul is prodigal of echoes. We may answer for the poetic faculty of its "maker." He is, in fact, not merely ingenious and fanciful, but abounds—the word with an allowance for the unhappiness of his subject, is scarcely too strong,—with passages of thoughtful sweetness and cheerful tenderness, at which we are constrained to smile and sigh, and both for "pastyme."

Was never payne but it had joye at last
In the fayre morrow.

There is a lovely cadence! And then Amour's courtship of his "swete ladie"—a "cynosure" before Milton's!—conducted as simply, yet touchingly, as if he were innocent of the seven deadly sciences, and knew no more of "the Ladye Grammere" than might become a troubadour:—

> O swete ladíe, the true and perfect star
> Of my true heart! Oh, take ye now pitíe!
> Think on my payne which am tofore you here—
> With your swete eyes behold you me, and see
> How thought and woe by great extremitíe
> Hath changed my colour into pale and wan!
> It was not so when I to love began.

The date assigned to this "Pastyme of Plesure" is 1506, some fifty years before the birth of Spenser. Whether it was written in vain for Spenser, judge ye! To the present generation it is covered deep with the dust of more than three centuries, and few tongues ask above the place,—"what lies here?"

Barclay is our next swan; and verily might be mistaken, in any sort taken, by naturalists, for a crow. He is our first writer of eclogues, the translator of the "Ship of Fools," and a thinker of his own thoughts with sufficient intrepidity.

Skelton "floats double, swan and shadow," as poet laureate of the University of Oxford, and "royal orator" of Henry VII. He presents a strange specimen of a court-poet, and if, as Erasmus says, "Britannicarum literarum lumen" at the same time,—the light is a pitchy torchlight, wild and rough. Yet we do not despise Skelton: despise him? it were easier to hate. The man is very strong; he triumphs, foams, is rabid, in the sense of strength; he mesmerizes our souls with the sense of strength—it is as easy to despise a wild beast in the forest, as John Skelton, poet laureate. He is as like a wild beast, as a poet laureate can be. In his wonderful dominion over language, he tears it, as with teeth and paws, ravenously, savagely: devasting rather than creating, dominant rather for liberty than for dignity. It is the very *sans-culottism* of eloquence; the oratory of a Silenus drunk with anger only. Mark him as the satyr of poets! fear him as the Juvenal of satyrs! and watch him with his rugged, rapid, picturesque savageness, his "breathless rhymes," to use the fit phrase of the satirist Hall, or—

> His rhymes all ragged,
> Tattered, and jagged,

to use his own,—climbing the high trees of Delphi, and pelting from thence his victim underneath, whether priest or cardinal, with rough-rinded apples! And then ask, could he write otherwise than so? The answer is this opening to his poem of the "Bouge of Court," and the impression inevitable, of the serious sense of beauty and harmony to which it gives evidence.

> In autumn when the sun *in virgine*
> By radiant heat enripened hath our corne,
> When Luna, full of mutabilitie,
> As empëress, the diadem hath worne
> Of our pole Arctic, smiling as in scorn
> At our folie and our unstedfastnesse—

but our last word of Skelton must be, that we do not doubt his influence for good upon our language. He was a writer singularly fitted for beating out the knots of the cordage, and straining the lengths to extension; a rough worker at rough work. Strong, rough Skelton! We can no more deride him than my good lord cardinal could. If our critical eyebrows must motion contempt at somebody of the period, we choose Tusser, and his five hundred points of good husbandry and housewifery. Whatever we say of Tusser, no fear of harming a poet,—

> Make ready a bin
> For chaff to lie in,

and there may be room *therein*, in compliment to the author of the proposition, for his own verses.

Lord Surrey passes as the tuner of our English nearly up to its present pitch of delicacy and smoothness; and we admit that he had a melody in his thoughts which they dared not disobey. That he is, as has been alleged by a chief critic, "our first metrical writer," lies not in our creed; and even Tuberville's more measured praise,—

> Our mother tongue by him hath got such lyght,
> That ruder speche thereby is banisht qwyht,—

we have difficulty in accepting. We venture to

be of opinion that he did not belong to that order of master-minds, with whom transitions originate, although qualified, by the quickness of a yielding grace, to assist effectually a transitional movement. There are names which catch the proverbs of praise as a hedge-thorn catches sheep's wool, by position and approximation rather than adaptitude: and this name is of them. Yet it is a high name. His poetry makes the ear lean to it, it is so sweet and low; the English he made it of, being ready to be sweet, and falling ripe in sweetness into other hands than his. For the poems of his friend, Sir Thomas Wyatt, have more thought, freedom, and variety, more general earnestness, more of the attributes of masterdom, than Lord Surrey's; while it were vain to reproach for lack of melody the writer of that loveliest lyric, "My lute, be still." And Wyatt is various in metres, and the first song-writer (that praise we must secure to him) of his generation. For the rest, there is an inequality in the structure of his verses which is very striking and observable in Surrey himself: as if the language, consciously insecure in her position, were balancing her accentual being and the forms of her pronunciation, half giddily, on the very turning point of transition. Take from Wyatt such a stanza as this, for instance,—

> The long love that in my thoughts I harbour
> And in my heart doth keep his residence,
> Into my face presseth with bold pretence,
> And there campeth, displaying his banner.

and oppose to it the next example, polished as Pope,—

> But I am here in Kent and Christendom,
> Among the Muses where I read and rhyme ;
> Where, if thou list, mine own John Poins, to come,
> Thou shalt be judge how I do spend my time.

It is well to mark Wyatt as a leader in the art of didactic poetic composition under the epistolary form, "sternly milde" (as Surrey said of his countenance) in the leaning toward satire. It is very well to mark many of his songs as of exceeding beauty, and as preserving clear their touching simplicity from that of over-curious conceits which infest his writings generally. That was the plague of Italian literature transmitted by contagion, together with better things —together with the love of love-lore, and the sonnet structure, the summer-bower for one fair thought, delighted in and naturalized in England by Wyatt and Surrey. For the latter,—

> From Tuscane came his ladye's worthy race:

and his Muse as well as his Geraldine. Drops from Plato's cup, passing through Petrarch's, not merely perfumed and colored but diluted by the medium, we find in Surrey's cup also. We must not underpraise Surrey to balance the overpraise we murmur at. Denying him supremacy as a reformer, the denial of his poetic nobleness is far from us. We attribute to him the chivalry of the *light* ages; we call him a scholastic troubadour. The longest and most beautiful of his poems ("describing the lover's whole state") was a memory in the mind of Milton when he wrote his Allegro. He has that measure of pathos whose expression is no gesture of passion, but the skilful fingering on a well-tuned lute. He affects us at worst not painfully, and

> With easie sighs such as folks draw in love.

He wrote the first English blank verse, in his translation of two books of the Æneid. He leads, in seeming, to the ear of the world, and by predestination of "popular breath," that little choral swan-chant which, swelled by Wyatt, Vaux, Bryan, and others, brake the common air in the days of the eighth Henry. And he fulfilled in sorrow his awarded fate as a poet, his sun going down at noon—and the cleft head, with its fair youthful curls, testifying like that fabled head of Orpheus, to the music of the living tongue.

Sackville, Lord Dorset, takes up the new blank verse from the lips of Surrey, and turns it to its right use of tragedy. We cannot say that he does for it much more. His "Gorboduc," with some twenty years between it and Shakespeare, is farther from the true drama in versification and all the rest, than "Gammer Gurton" is from "Gorboduc." Sackville's blank verse, like Lord

Surrey's before him, is only heroic verse without rhyme: and we must say so in relation to Gascoigne, who wrote the second blank verse tragedy, the "Jocasta," and the first blank verse original poem, "The Stele Glass." The secret of the blank verse of Shakespeare, and Fletcher, and Milton, did not dwell with them: the arched cadence, with its artistic key-stone and underflood of broad continuous sound, was never achieved nor attempted by its first builders. We sometimes whisper in our silence that Marlowe's "brave sublunary" instincts should have groped that way. But no! Chaucer had more sense of music in the pause than Marlowe had. Marlowe's rhythm is not, indeed, hard and stiff and uniform, like the sentences of "Gorboduc," as if the pattern-one had been cut in boxwood: there is a difference between uniformity and monotony, and he found it; his cadence revolves like a wheel, progressively if slowly and heavily, and with an orbicular grandeur of unbroken and unvaried music.

It remains to us to speak of the work by which Sackville is better known than by "Gorboduc,"—the "Mirror for Magistrates." The design of it has been strangely praised, seeing that whatever that peculiar merit were, Lydgate's "Fall of Princes" certainly cast the shadow before. But Sackville's commencement of the execution proved the master's hand; and that the great canvas fell abandoned to the blurring brushes of inadequate disciples, was an ill-fortune compensated adequately by the honor attributed to the Induction—of inducing a nobler genius than his own, even Spenser's, to a nobler labor. We cannot doubt the influence of that Induction. Its colossal figures, in high allegorical relief, were exactly adapted to impress the outspread fancy of the most sensitive of poets. A yew-tree cannot stand at noon in an open pleasaunce without throwing the outline of its branches on the broad and sunny grass. Still, admitting the suggestion in its fulness, nothing can differ more than the allegorical results of the several geniuses of Lord Dorset and Spenser. Tear-drop and dew-drop, respond more similarly to analysis; or morbid grief and ideal joy. Sackville stands close wrapt in the "blanket of his dark," and will not drop his mantle for the sun. Spenser's business is with the lights of the world, and the lights beyond the world.

But this Sackville, this Earl of Dorset, ("Oh, a fair earl was he!") stands too low for admeasurement with Spenser: and we must look back, if covetous of comparisons, to some one of a loftier and more kingly stature. We must look back far, and stop at Chaucer. Spenser and Chaucer do naturally remind us of each other, they two being the most cheerful-hearted of the poets—with whom cheerfulness, as an attribute of poetry, is scarcely a common gift. But the world will be upon us! The world moralizes of late and in its fashion, upon the immorality of mournful poems, upon the criminality of "melodious tears," upon the morbidness of the sorrows of poets,—because Lord Byron was morbidly sorrowful, and because a crowd of his ephemeral imitators hung their heads all on one side and were sincerely sorrowful. The fact, however, has been, apart from Lord Byron and his disciples, that the "*ai αι*" of Apollo's flower is vocally sad in the prevailing majority of poetical compositions. The philosophy is, perhaps, that the poetic temperament, halfway between the light of the ideal and the darkness of the real, and rendered by each more sensitive to the other, and unable, without a struggle, to pass out clear and calm into either, bears the impress of the necessary conflict in dust and blood. The philosophy may be, that only the stronger spirits do accomplish this victory, having lordship over their own genius; whether they accomplish it by looking bravely to the good ends of evil things, which is the practical ideal, and possible to all men in a measure—or by abstracting the inward sense from sensual things and their influences, which is subjectivity perfected—or by glorifying sensual things with the inward sense, which is objectivity transfigured—or by attaining to the highest vision of the idealist, which is subjectivity turned outward into an actual objectivity.

To the last triumph, Shakespeare attained; but Chaucer and Spenser fulfilled their destiny and grew to their mutual likeness as cheerful poets, by certain of the former processes. They two are alike in their cheerfulness, yet are their cheerfulnesses most unlike. Each poet laughs: yet their laughters ring with as far a difference as the sheep-bell on the hill and the joy-bell in the city. Each is earnest in his gladness: each active in persuading you of it. You are persuaded, and hold each for a cheerful man. The whole difference is, that Chaucer has a cheerful humanity: Spenser a cheerful ideality. One, rejoices walking on the sunny side of the street: the other walking out of the street in a way of his own, kept green by a blessed vision. One, uses the adroitness of his fancy by distilling out of the visible universe her occult smiles: the other, by fleeing beyond the possible frown, the occasions of natural ills, to that "cave of cloud" where he may smile safely to himself. One, holds festival with men—seldom so coarse and loud indeed, as to startle the deer from their green covert at Woodstock—or with homely Nature and her "douce Marguerite" low in the grasses: the other adopts, for his playfellows, imaginary or spiritual existences, and will not say a word to Nature herself, unless it please her to dress for his masque and speak daintily sweet and rare like a spirit. The human heart of one utters oracles; the imagination of the other speaks for his heart, and we miss no prophecy. For music, we praised Chaucer's, and not only as Dryden did, for a "Scotch tune." But never issued there from lip or instrument, or the tuned causes of nature, more lovely sound than we gather from our Spenser's Art. His mouth is vowed away from the very possibilities of harshness. Right leans to wrong in its excess. His rhythm is the continuity of melody, not harmony, because too smooth for modulation—because "by his vow" he dares not touch a discord for the sake of consummating a harmony. It is the singing of an angel in a dream: it has not enough of contrary for waking music. Of his great poem we may say, that we miss no humanity in it, because we make a new humanity out of it and are satisfied in our human hearts—a new humanity vivified by the poet's life, moving in happy measure to the chanting of his thoughts, and upon ground supernaturally beautified by his sense of the beautiful. As an allegory, it enchants us away from his own purposes. Una is Una to us; and Sans Foy is a traitor, and Error is "an ugly monster," with a "tayle;" and we thank nobody in the world, not even Spenser, for trying to prove it otherwise. Do we dispraise an allegorical poem by throwing off its allegory? we trow not. Probably, certainly to our impression, the highest triumph of an allegory, from this of the "Faery Queen" down to the "Pilgrim's Progress," is the abnegation of itself.

O those days of Elizabeth! We call them the days of Elizabeth, but the glory fell over the ridge, in illustration of the half-century beyond: those days of Elizabeth! Full were they of poets as the summer-days are of birds,—

> No branch on which a fine bird did not sit,
> No bird but his sweet song did shrilly sing,
> No song but did contayne a lovely dit.

We hear of the dramatists, and shall speak of

them presently; but the lyric singers were yet more numerous,—there were singers in every class. Never since the first nightingale brake voice in Eden, arose such a jubilee-concert: never before nor since has such a crowd of true poets uttered true poetic speech in one day. Not in England evermore! Not in Greece, that we know. Not in Rome, by what we know. Talk of their Augustan era—we will not talk of it, lest we desecrate our own of Elizabeth. The latter was rightly prefigured by our figure of the chorus of swans. It was besides the milky way of poetry: it was the miracle-age of poetical history. We may fancy that the master-souls of Shakespeare and Spenser, breathing, stirring in divine emotion, shot vibratory life through other souls in electric association: we may hear in fancy, one wind moving every leaf in a forest—one voice responded to by a thousand rock-echoes. Why, a common man walking through the earth in those days, grew a poet by position—even as a child's shadow cast upon a mountain slope is dilated to the aspect of a giant's.

If we, for our own parts, did enact a Briareus, we might count these poets on the fingers of our hundred hands, after the fashion of the poets of Queen Anne's time, counting their syllables. We do not talk of them as "faultless monsters," however wonderful in the multitude and verity of their gifts: their faults were numerous, too. Many poets of an excellent sweetness, thinking of poetry that, like love,

> It was to be all made of fantasy,—

fell poetry-sick, as they might fall love-sick, and knotted associations, far and free enough to girdle the earth withal, into true love-knots of quaintest devices. Many poets affected novelty rather than truth; and many attained to novelty rather by attitude than altitude, whether of thought or word. Worst of all, many were incompetent to Sir Philip Sidney's ordeal—the translation of their verses into prose—and would have perished utterly by that hot ploughshare. Still, the natural healthy eye turns toward the light, and the true calling of criticism remains the distinguishing of beauty.

Love and honor to the poets of Elizabeth—honor and love to them all! Honor even to the fellow-workers with Sackville in the "Mirror for Magistrates," to Ferrers, Churchyard, and others, who had their hand upon the ore if they did not clasp it! and to Warner, the poet of Albion's England, singing snatches of ballad-pathos, while he worked for the most part heavily, too, with a bowed back as at a stiff soil—and to Gascoigne, reflecting beauty and light from his "Stele Glass," though his "Fruites of War" are scarcely fruits from Parnassus—and to Daniel, tender and noble, and teaching, in his "Musophilus," the chivalry of poets, though in his "Civil Wars," somewhat too historical, as Drayton has written of him—and to Drayton, generous in the "Polyolbion" of his poet-blessing on every hill and river through this fair England, and not ineloquent in his Heroical Epistles, though somewhat tame and level in his "Barons' Wars"—and to the two brother Fletchers, Giles and Phineas, authors of "Christ's Victory" and "The Purple Island," for whom the Muse's kiss followed close upon the mother's, gifting their lips with no vulgar music and their house with that noble kinsman, Fletcher the dramatist! Honor, too, to Davies, who "reasoned in verse" with a strong mind and strong enunciation, though he wrote one poem on the Soul and another on Dancing, and concentrated the diverging rays of intellect and folly in his sonnets on the reigning Astræa—and to Fulke Greville, Lord Brooke, who had deep thoughts enough to accomplish ten poets of these degenerate days, though because of some obscurity in their expression you would find some twenty critics "full of oaths" by the pyramids, that they all meant nothing—and to Chamberlayne, picturesque, imaginative, earnest (by no means dramatic) in his poetic romance of "Pharonnida," though accumulative to excess of figures, and pedantic in such verbal learning as "entheon charms," the "catagraph" of a picture, the "exagitations and congestions of elements," *et sic omnia!*—to Chalkhill, wrapt, even bound, "in soft Lydian airs," till himself, as well as his Clearchus and Thealma, fall asleep in involutions of harmony—and to Browne, something languid in his "Britannia's Pastorals," by sitting in the sun with Guarini and Marini, and "perplext in the extreme" by a thousand images and sounds of beauty calling him across the dewy fields—and to Wither, author of the "Shepherd's Hunting," and how much else? Wither, who wrote of poetry like a poet, and in return has been dishonored and misprised by some of his own kind—a true sincere poet of blessed oracles! Honor, love, and praise to him and all! May pardon come to us from the unnamed.

Honor also to the translators of poems—to such as Chapman and Sylvester—great hearts, interpreters of great hearts, and afterwards worthily thanked by the Miltons, and Popes, and Keats's, for their gift of greatness to the language of their England.

Honor to the satirists! to Marston, who struck boldly and coarsely at an offence from the same level with the offender—to Hall, preserving his own elevation, and flashing downwardly those thick lightnings in which we smell the sulphur—and to Donne, whose instinct to beauty overcame the resolution of his satiric humor.

Honor, again, to the singers of brief poems, to the lyrists and sonnetteers! O Shakespeare, let thy name rest gently among them, perfuming the place. We "swear" that these sonnets and songs do verily breathe, "not of themselves, but *thee;*" and we recognize and bless them as short sighs from thy large poetic heart, burdened with diviner inspirations! O rare Ben Jonson, let us have thy songs, rounded each with a spherical thought, and the lyrics from thy masques alive with learned fantasy, and thine epigrams keen and quaint, and thy noble epitaphs, under which the dead seem stirring! Fletcher, thou shalt be with us—prophet of Comus and Penseroso! giddy with inhalation from the fount of the beautiful, speaking out wildly thought upon thought, measure upon measure, as the bird sings, because his own voice is lovely to him. Sidney, true knight and fantastic poet, whose soul did too curiously inquire the fashion of the beautiful—the fashion rather than the secret,—but left us in one line, the completest "Ars Poetica" extant,—

> "Foole, sayde my Muse to mee, looke in thine heart,
> and write,—"

thy name be famous in all England and Arcadia! And Raleigh, tender and strong, of voice sweet enough to answer that "Passionate Shepherd," yet trumpet-shrill to speak the "Soul's errand" thrilling the depths of our own! having honor and suffering as became a poet, from the foot of the Lady of England light upon his cloak, to the cloak of his executioner wrapping redly his breathless corpse. Marlowe,—we must not forget his "Shepherd" in his tragedies: and "Come live with me" sounds passionately still through the dead cold centuries. And Drummond, the over-praised and under-praised,—a passive poet, if we may use the phraseology,—who was not careful to achieve greatness, but whose natural pulses beat music, and with whom the consciousness of life was the sentiment of beauty. And Lyly, shriven from the sins of his Euphues, with a quaint grace in his songs;

and Donne, who takes his place naturally in this new class, having a dumb angel, and knowing more noble poetry than he articulates. Herrick, the Ariel of poets, sucking "where the bee sucks" from the rose-heart of nature, and reproducing the fragrance idealized; and Carew, using all such fragrance as a courtly essence, with less of self-abandonment and more of artificial application; and Herbert, with his face as the face of a spirit, dimly bright; and fantastic Quarles, in rude and graphic gesticulation, expounding verity and glory; and Breton, and Turberville, and Lodge, and Hall (not the satirist), and all the hundred swans, nameless or too numerous to be named, of that Cayster of the rolling time.

Then, high in the miraculous climax, come the dramatists—from whose sinews was knit the overcoming strength of our literature over all the nations of the world. "The drama is the executive of literature," said De Staël: and the Greek's "action, action, action," we shall not miss in our drama. Honor to the dramatists, as honor from them!

We must take a few steps backward for position's sake, and then be satisfied with a rapid glance at the Drama. From the days of Norman William, the representations called Mysteries and Moralities had come and gone without a visible poet; and Skelton appears before us almost the first English claimant of a dramatic reputation, with the authorship of the interludes of "Magnificence" and the "Nigromansir." The latter is chiefly famous for Warton's affirmation of having held it in his hands, giving courteous occasion to Ritson's denial of its existence: and our own palms having never been crossed by the silver of either, we cannot prophesy on the degree of individual honor involved in the literary claim. Bale, one of the eighth Henry's bishops, was an active composer of Moralities; and John Heywood, his royal jester and "author of that very merry interlude" called *The Four P's*, united in his merriment that caustic sense with that lively ease, which have not been too common since in his accomplished dramatic posterity. Yet those who in the bewilderment of their admirations (or senses) attribute to John

Heywood the "Pinner of Wakefield," are more obviously—we are sorely tempted to add more ridiculously—wrong, than those who attribute it to Shakespeare. The Canon of Windsor's "Ralph Royster Doyster," and the Bishop of Bath and Wells's "Gammer Gurton," followed each other close into light, the earliest modern comedies, by the force of the "*âme ecclésiasti que.*" A little after came Ferrys, memorialized by Puttenham as "the principall man of his profession" (of poetry), and "of no lesse myrthe and felicitie than John Heywood, but of much more skille and magnificence in his meter." But seeing that even Oblivion forgot Ferrys, leaving his name and Puttenham's praise when she defaced his works, and seeing, too, the broad farcedom of the earlier, however episcopal writers, we find ourselves in an unwilling posture of recognition before Edwards, as the first extant regular dramatist of England. It is a pitiful beginning. *The Four P's* would be a more welcome A to us. They express more power with their inarticulate roughness, than does this Damon and Pythias, with its rhymed, loitering frigidity, or even than this Palamon and Arcite, in which the sound of the hunting horn cast into ecstasy the too gracious soul of Queen Elizabeth. But Sir John Davies's divine Astræa was, at that gray dawn of her day, ignorant of greater poets; and we ("happy in this") go on toward them. After Edwards, behold Sackville with that "Gorboduc" we have named, the first blank verse tragedy we can name, praised by Sidney for its exemplary preservation of the unities and for "climbing to the height of Seneca his stile,"—tight-fitting praise, considering that the composition is high enough to account for its snow, and cold enough to emulate the Roman's. And after Sackville, behold the first dramatic geniuses, in juxtaposition with the first dramatists—Peele, and Kyd, mad as his own Hieronimo (we will grant it to such critics as are too utterly in their senses), only—

> When he is mad,
> Then, methinks, he is a brave fellow!

and then, methinks, and by such madness, the possibility of a Shakespeare was revealed. Kyd's blank verse is probably the first breaking of the true soil; and certainly far better and more dramatic than Marlowe's is,—crowned poet as the latter stands before us—poet of the English Faustus, which we will not talk of against the German, nor set up its grand, luxurious, melancholy devil against Goethe's subtle, biting, Voltairish devil, each being devil after its kind,—the poet of the Jew which Shakespeare drew (not), yet a true Jew "with a berde,"—and the poet of the first historical drama,—since the "Gorboduc" scarcely can be called one. Marlowe was more essentially a poet than a dramatist; and if the remark appear self-evident and universally applicable, we will take its reverse in Kyd, who was more essentially, with all his dramatic faults, a dramatist than a poet. Passing from the sound of the elemental monotonies of the rhythm of Marlowe, we cannot pause before Nash and Greene to distinguish their characteristics. It is enough to name these names of gifted dramatists, who lived, or at least wrote, rather before Shakespeare than with him, and helped to make him credible. Through them, like a lens, we behold his light. Of them we conjecture—these are the blind elements working before the earthquake,—before the great "Shakescene," as Greene said when he was cross. And we may say when we are fanciful, these are the experiments of Nature, made in her solution of the problem of how much deathless poetry will agree with how much mortal clay—these are the potsherd vessels half filled, and failing at last,—until up to the edge of *one*, the liquid inspiration rose and bubbled in hot beads to quench the thirsty lips of the world.

It is hard to speak of Shakespeare; these measures of the statures of common poets fall from our hands when we seek to measure him: it is harder to praise him. Like the tall plane-tree which Xerxes found standing in the midst of an open country, and honored inappropriately with his "barbaric pomp," with bracelets and chains and rings suspended on its branches, so has it been with Shakespeare. A thousand critics have commended him with praises as unsuitable as a gold ring to a plane-tree. A thousand hearts have gone out to him, carrying necklaces. Some have discovered that he individualized, and some that he generalized, and some that he subtilized—almost *trans*-transcendentally. Some would have it that he was a wild genius, sowing wild oats and stealing deer to the end, with no more judgment forsooth than "youth the hare;" and some, that his very pulses beat by that critical law of art in which he was blameless:—some, that all his study was in his horn-book, and not much of that; and some, that he was as learned a polyglott as ever had been dull but for Babel:—some, that his own ideal burned steadfastly within his own fixed contemplations, unstirred by breath from without; and some, that he wrote for the gold on his palm and the "rank popular breath" in his nostrils, apart from consciousness of greatness and desire of remembrance. If the opinions prove nothing, their contradictions prove the exaltation of the object; their contradictions are praise. For men differ about things above their reach, not within it;—about the mountains in the moon, not Primrose hill: and more than seven cities of men have differed in their talk about Homer also. Homer, also, was convicted of indiscreet nodding; and Homer, also, had no manner of judgment, and the Ars Poetica people could not abide his bad taste. And we find another analogy. We, who have no leaning to the popular cant of Romanticism and Classicism, and believe the old Greek BEAUTY to be both new and old, and as alive and not more gray in Webster's "Dutchess of Malfy" than in Æschylus's "Eumenides," do reverence this Homer and this Shakespeare as the colossal borderers of the two intellectual departments of the world's age,—do behold from their feet the antique and modern literatures sweep outwardly away, and conclude, that whereas the Greek bore in his depth the seed and prophecy of all the Hellenic and Roman poets, so did Shakespeare "whose seed was in himself" also, those of a later generation.

For the rest we must speak briefly of Shakespeare, and very weakly too, except for love. That he was a great natural genius nobody, we believe, has doubted—the fact has passed with the cheer of mankind; but that he was a great artist the majority has doubted. Yet Nature and Art cannot be reasoned apart into antagonistic principles. Nature is God's art—the accomplishment of a spiritual significance hidden in a sensible symbol. Poetic art (man's) looks past the symbol with a divine guess and reach of soul into the mystery of the significance,—disclosing from the analysis of the visible things, the synthesis or unity of the ideal,—and expounds like symbol and like significance out of the infinite of God's doing into the finite of man's comprehending. Art lives by Nature, and not the bare mimetic life generally attributed to Art: she does not imitate, she expounds. *Interpres naturæ*—is the poet-artist; and the poet wisest in nature is the most artistic poet: and thus our Shakespeare passes to the presidency unquestioned, as the greatest artist in the world. We believe in his judgment as in his genius. We believe in his learning, both of books and men, and hills and valleys: in his grammars and dictionaries we do not believe. In his philosophy of language we believe absolutely: in his Babel-learning, not at all. We believe reverently in the miracle of his variety; and it is observable that we become aware of it less by the numerousness of his persons and their positions, than by the *depth* of the least of either,—by the sense of visibility beyond what we see, as in nature. Our creed goes on to declare him most passionate and most rational—of an emotion which casts us into thought, of a reason which leaves us open to emotion: most grave and most gay—while we scarcely can guess that the man Shakespeare is grave or gay, because he interposes between ourselves and his personality the whole breadth and length of his ideality. His associative faculty, —the wit's faculty besides the poet's—for him who was both wit and poet, shed sparks like an electric wire. He was wise in the world, having studied it in his heart; what is called "the knowledge of the world" being just the knowledge of one heart, and certain exterior symbols. What else? What otherwise could he, the young transgressor of Sir Thomas Lucy's fences, new from Stratford and the Avon, close in the atric London, have seen or touched or handled of the Hamlets and Lears and Othellos, that he should draw them? "How can I take portraits," said Marmontel, in a similar inexperience, "before I have beheld faces?" Voltaire embraced him, in reply. Well applauded, Voltaire! It was a *mot* for Marmontel's utterance, and Voltaire's praise—for Marmontel, not for Shakespeare. Every being is his own centre to the universe, and in himself must one foot of the compasses be fixed to attain to any measurement: nay, every being is his own mirror to the universe. Shakespeare wrote from within—the beautiful; and we recognize from within—the true. He is universal, because he is individual. And without any prejudice of admiration, we may go on to account his faults to be the proofs of his power; the cloud of dust cast up by the multitude of the chariots. The activity of his associative faculty is occasionally morbid: in the abundance of his winged thoughts, the locust flies with the bee, and the ground is dark with the shadow of them. Take faults, take excellences, it is impossible to characterize this Shakespeare by an epithet: have we heard the remark before, that it should sound so obvious? We say of Corneille, the noble; of Racine, the tender; of Æschylus, the terrible; of Sophocles, the perfect; but not one of these words, not one appropriately descriptive epithet, can we attach to Shakespeare without a conscious recoil. Shakespeare! the name is the description.

He is the most wonderful artist in blank verse of all in England, and almost the earliest. We do not say that he first broke the enchaining monotony, of which the Sackvilles and the Marlowes left us complaining; because the versification of "Hieronimo" ran at its own strong will, and the "Pinner of Wakefield" may have preceded his first plays. We do not even say what we might, that his hand first proved the compass and infinite modulation of the new instrument; but we do say, that it never answered another hand as it answered his. We do say, this fingering was never learned of himself by another. From Massinger's more resonant majesty, from even Fletcher's more numerous and artful cadences, we turn back to his artlessness of art, to his singular and supreme estate as a versificator. Often when he is at the sweetest, his words are poor monosyllables, his pauses frequent to brokenness, and the structure of the several lines less varied than was taught after Fletcher's masterdom; but the whole results in an ineffable charming of the ear which we acquiesce in without seeking its cause, a happy mystery of music.

This is little for Shakespeare; yet so much for the place, that we are forced into brevities for our observations which succeed. We chronicle only the names of Chapman, Dekker, Webster, Tourneur, Randolph, Middleton, and Thomas Heywood, although great names, and worthy, it is not too much to add, of Shakespeare's brotherhood. Many besides lean from our memory to the paper, but we put them away reverently. It was the age of the dramatists—the age of strong passionate men, scattering on every side their good and evil oracles of vehement humanity, and extenuating no thought in its word: and in that age, "to write like a man," was a deed accomplished by many besides him of whom it was spoken, Jonson's "son Cartwright."

At Jonson's name we stop perforce, and do salutation in the dust to the impress of that "learned sock." He was a learned man, as everybody knows; and as everybody does not believe, not the worse for his learning. His material, brought laboriously from East and West, is wrapt in a flame of his own. If the elasticity and abandonment of Shakespeare and of certain of Shakespeare's brothers, are not found in his writings, the reason of the defects need not be sought out in his readings. His genius, high and verdant as it grew, yet belonged to the hard woods: it was lance-wood rather than bow-wood—a genius rather noble than graceful—eloquent, with a certain severity and emphasis of enunciation. It would have been the same if he, too, had known "little Latin and lesse Greek." There was a dash of the rhetorical in his dramatic. Not that we deny him empire over the passions: his heart had rhetoric as well as his understanding, and he wrote us a "Sad Shepherd," as well as a "Catiline." His versification heaves heavily with thought. For his comic powers, let "Volpone" and "The Alchymist" attest them with that unextinguishable laughter which is the laughter of gods or poets still more than of the wit's coffee-house. Was it "done at the Mermaid," was it ever fancied there, that "rare Ben Jonson" should be called a pedantic poet? Nay, but only a scholastic one.

And Beaumont and Fletcher, the Castor and Pollux of this starry poetic sphere, (*lucida sidera!*) our silence shall not cover them; nor will we put asunder, in our speech, the names which friendship and poetry joined together, nor distinguish, by a labored analysis, the vivacity of one from the solidity of the other; seeing that men who, according to tradition, lived in one house, and wore one cloak, and wrote on one page, may well, by the sanctity of that one grave they have also in common, maintain forever beyond it the unity they coveted. The characteristics of these writers stand out in a softened light from the deep tragic background of the times. We may liken them to Shakespeare in one mood of his mind, because there are few classes of beauty, the type or likeness of which is not discoverable in Shakespeare. From the rest they stand out contrastingly, as the Apollo of the later Greek sculpture-school,—too graceful for divinity and too vivacious for marble,—placed in a company of the antiquer statues with their grand blind look of the almightiness of repose. We cannot say of these poets as of the rest, "they write all like men;" we cannot think they write like women either: perhaps they write a little like centaurs. We are of opinion in any way, that the grace is more obvious than the strength; and there may be something centauresque and of twofold nature in their rushing mutabilities, and changes on passion and weakness. Clearest of all is that they wrote like poets, and in a versification most surpassingly musical though liberal, as if music served them for love's sake, unbound! They had an excellent genius, but not a strong enough invention to include judgment; judgment being the consistency of invention, and consistency always, whether in morals or literature, depending upon strength. We do not, in fact, find in them any perfect and covenanted whole—we do not find it in character, or in plot, or in composition; and lamenting the defect on many grounds we do so on this chief one, that their good is just good, their evil just evil, unredeemed into good like Shakespeare's and Nature's evil by unity of design, but lying apart, a willingly chosen, through and through evil—and "by this time it stinketh." If other results are less lamentable they are no less fatal. The mirror which these poets held up to us is vexed with a thousand cracks, and every thing visible is in fragments. Their conceptions all tremble on a peradventure—"peradventure they shall do well;" there is no royal absolute will that they should do well: the poets are less kings than workmen. And being workmen they are weak —the moulds fall from their hands—are clutched with a spasm or fall with a faintness. After which querulousness, we shall leave the question as to whether their tragic or comic powers be put to more exquisite use,—not for solution, nor for doubt (since we hold fast an opinion), but for praise the most rarely appropriate or possible.

One passing word of Ford, the pathetic—for he may wear on his sleeve the epithet of Euripides, and no daw peck there. Most tender is he, yet not to feebleness—most mournful, yet not to languor; yet we like to hear the war-horse leaps of Dekker on the same tragic ground with him, producing at once contrast and completeness. Ungrateful thought!—the "Witch of Edmonton" bewitched us to it. Ford can fill the ear and soul singly, with the trumpet-note of his pathos; and in its pauses you shall hear the murmuring voices of nature,—such a nightingale, for instance, as never sang on a common night. Then that death scene in the "Broken Heart!" who has equalled *that?* It is single in the drama,—the tragic of tragedy and the sublime of grief. A word, too, of Massinger, who writes all like a giant—a dry-eyed giant. He is too ostentatiously strong for flexibility, and too heavy for rapidity, and monotonous through his perpetual final trochee; his gesture and enunciation are slow and majestic. And another word of Shirley, an inferior writer, though touched, to our fancy, with something of a finer ray, and closing, in worthy purple, the procession of the Elizabethan men. Shirley is the last dramatist. *Valete et plaudite, o posteri.*

Standing in his traces, and looking backward and before, we become aware of the distinct demarcations of five eras of English poetry: the first, the Chaucerian, although we might call it *Chaucer;* the second, the Elizabethan; the third, which culminates in Cowley; the fourth, in Dryden and the French school; the fifth, the return to nature in Cowper and his successors of our day. These five rings mark the age of the fair and stingless serpent we are impelled, like the ancient mariner, to bless—but not "unaware." "*Ah benedicite!*" we bless her so, out of our Chaucer's rubric, softly, but with a plaintiveness of pleasure. For when the last echo of the Elizabethan harmonies had died away with Shirley's footsteps, in the twilight of that golden day; when Habington and Lovelace, and every last bird before nightfall was dumb, and Crashaw's fine rapture, holy as a summer sense of silence, left us to the stars—the first voices startling the thinker from his reverting thoughts, are verily of another spirit. The voices are eloquent enough, thoughtful enough, fanciful enough; but something is defective. Can any one suffer, as an experimental reader, the transition between the second and third periods, without feeling that something is defective? What is so? And who dares to guess that it may be INSPIRATION?

"Poetry is of too spiritual a nature," Mr. Campbell has observed, "to admit of its authors being exactly grouped by a Linnæan system of classification." Nevertheless, from those subtle influences which poets render and receive, and from other causes less obvious but no less operative, it has resulted even to ourselves in this slight survey of the poets of our country, that the signs used by us simply as signs of historical demarcation, have naturally fallen or risen into signs of poetical classification. The five eras we spoke of just now, have indeed each a characteristic as clear in poetry as in chronology; and a deeper gulf than an *Anno Domini* yawns betwixt an Elizabethan man and a man of that third era upon which we are entering. The change of the poetical characteristic was not, indeed, without gradation. The hands of the clock had been moving silently for a whole hour before the new one struck; and even in Davies, even in Drayton, we felt the cold foreshadow of a change. The word "sweetness," which presses into our sentences against the will of our rhetoric whenever we speak of Shakespeare ("sweetest Shakespeare") or his kin, we lose the taste of in the later waters; they are brackish with another age.

In what did the change consist? Practically and partially in the idol-worship of *rhyme.* Among the elder poets, the rhyme was only a felicitous adjunct, a musical accompaniment, the tinkling of a cymbal through the choral harmonies. You heard it across the changes of the pause, as an undertone of the chant, marking the time with an audible indistinctness, and catching occasionally and reflecting the full light of the emphasis of the sense in mutual elucidation. But the new practice endeavored to identify in all possible cases the rhyme and what may be called the sentimental emphasis; securing the latter to the tenth rhyming *syllable*, and so dishonoring the emphasis of the sentiment into the base use of the marking of the time. And not only by this unnatural provision did the emphasis minister to the rhyme, but the pause did it also. "Away with all pauses,"—said the reformers,—"except the legitimate pause at the tenth rhyming syllable. O rhyme, live forever! Rhyme alone take the incense from our altars,—tinkling cymbal alone be our music!" —And so arose, in dread insignificance, the Heart-and-impart men.

Moreover, the corruption of the versification was but a type of the change in the poetry itself, and sufficiently expressive. The accession to the throne of the poets, of the *wits* in the new current sense of the term, or of the beaux esprits—a term to be used the more readily because descriptive of the actual pestilential influence of French literature—was accompanied by the substitution of elegant thoughts for poetic conceptions ("elegant" alas! beginning to be the critical pass-word), of adroit illustrations for beautiful images, of ingenuity for genius. Yet this third era is only the preparation for the fourth consummating one—the hesitation before the crime: we smell the blood through it in the bath-room. And our fancy grows hysterical, like poor Octavia, while the dismal extent of the "quantum mutatus" develops itself in detail.

"Waller's sweetness!" it is a needy antithesis to Denham's strength,—and, if any thing beside, a sweetness as far removed from that which we have lately recognized, as the saccharine of the palate from the melodious of the ear. Will Saccharissa frown at our comparison from the high sphere of his verse? or will she, a happy "lady who can sleep when she pleases," please to oversleep our offence? It is certain that we but walk in her footsteps in our disdain of her poet, even if we disdain him—and most seriously we disown any such partaking of her "crueltie." Escaping from the first astonishment of an unhappy transition, and from what is still more vexing, those "base, common, and popular" critical voices, which, in and out of various "arts of poetry," have been pleased to fix upon this same transitional epoch as the genesis of excellence to our language and versification, we do not, we hope it of ourselves, undervalue Waller. There is a certain grace "beyond the reach of art," or rather beyond the destructive reach of his ideas of art, to which, we opine, if he had not been a courtier and a renegade, the Lady Dorothea might have bent her courtly head unabashed, even as the Penshurst beeches did. We gladly acknowledge in him, as in Denham and other poets of the transition, an occasional remorseful recurrence by half lines and whole lines, or even a few lines together, to the poetic Past. We will do any thing but agree with Mr. Hallam, who, in his excellent and learned work on the Literature of Europe, has passed some singular judgments upon the poets, and none more startling than his comparison of Waller to Milton, on the ground of the sustenance of power. The crying truth is louder than Mr. Hallam, and cries, in spite of Fame, with whom poor Waller was an "enfant trouvé," an heir by chance, rather than merit,—that he is feeble poetically quite as surely as morally and politically, and that, so far from being an equal and sustained poet, he has not strength for unity even in his images, nor for continuity in his thoughts, nor for adequacy in his expression, nor for harmony in his versification. This is at least our strong and sustained impression of Edmund Waller.

With a less natural gift of poetry than Waller, Denham has not only more strength of purpose and language (an easy superiority), but some strength in the abstract: he puts forth rather a sinewy hand to the new structure of English versification. It is true, indeed, that in his only poem which survives to any competent popularity—his "Cooper's Hill"—we may find him again and again, by an instinct to a better principle, receding to the old habit of the medial pause, instead of the would-be sufficiency of the final one. But, generally, he is true to his modern sect of the Pharisees; and he helps their prosperity otherwise by adopting that pharisaic fashion of setting forth, vain-gloriously, a little virtue of thought and poetry in pointed and antithetic expression, which all the wits delighted in, from himself, a chief originator, to Pope, the perfecter. The famous lines, inheriting by entail a thousand critical admirations—

> "Strong without rage, without o'erflowing full,"

and as Sydney Smith might put it, "a great many other things without a great many other things," contain the germ and prophecy of the whole Queen Anne's generation. For the rest, we will be brief in our melancholy, and say no more of Denham than that he was a Dryden *in small.*

The genius of the new school was its anomaly, even Abraham Cowley. We have said nothing of "the metaphysical poets," because we disclaim the classification, and believe with Mr. Leigh Hunt, that every poet, inasmuch as he is a poet, is a metaphysician. In taking note, therefore, of this Cowley, who stands on the very vibratory soil of the transition, and stretches his faltering and protesting hands on either side to the old and to the new, let no one brand him for "metaphysics." He was a true poet, both by natural constitution and cultivation, but without the poet's heart. His admirers have compared him to Pindar; and, taking Pindar out of his rapture, they may do so still: he was a Pindar writing by *métier* rather than by *verve*. In rapidity and subtlety of the associate faculty, which, however, with him, moved circularly rather than onward, he was sufficiently Pindaric: but, as it is a fault in the Greek lyrist to leave his buoyancy to the tumultous rush of his associations too unmisgivingly and entirely for the right reverence of Unity in Beauty,—so is it the crime of the English poet to commit coldly what the other permitted passively, and with a conscious volition, quick yet calm, calm when quickest, to command from the ends of the universe the associations of material sciences and spiritual philosophies. Quickness of the associative or suggestive faculty is common, we have had occasion to observe, to the wit (in the modern sense) and the poet; its application only, being of a reverse difference. Cowley confounded the application, and became a witty poet. The Elizabethan writers were inclined to a too curious illuminating of thought, by imagery. Cowley was coarsely curious: he went to the shambles for his chambers of imagery, and very often through the mud. All which faults appear to us attributable to his coldness of temperament, and his defectiveness in the instinct towards Beauty; to having the intellect only of a great poet, not the sensibility. His "Davideis," our first epic in point of time, has fine things in it. His translations, or rather paraphrases of Anacreon, are absolutely the most perfect of any English composition of their order. His other poems contain profuse material, in image and reflection, for the accomplishment of three poets, each greater than himself. He approached the beautiful and the true as closely as mere Fancy could; but that very same Fancy, unfixed by feeling, too often, in the next breath, approximated him to the hideous and the false. Noble thoughts are in Cowley—we say noble, and we might say sublime; but, while we speak, he falls below the first praise. Yet his influence was for good rather than for evil, by inciting to a struggle backward, a delay in the revolutionary movement: and this, although a wide gulf yawned between him and the former age, and his heart's impulse was not strong enough to cast him across it. For his actual influence, he lifts us up and casts us down—charms, and goes nigh to disgust us—does all but make us love and weep.

And then came "glorious John," with the whole fourth era in his arms;—and eloquent above the sons of men, to talk down, thunder down poetry as it were an exhalation. Do we speak as if he were not a poet? nay, but we speak of the character of his influences; nay, but he was a poet—an excellent poet—in marble: and Phidias, with the sculpturesque ideal separated from his working tool, might have carved him. He was a poet without passion, just as Cowley was: but then, Cowley lived by fancy, and that would have been poor living for

John Dryden. Unlike Cowley, too, he had an earnestness which of itself was influential. He was inspired in his understanding and his senses only; but to the point of disenchanting the world most marvellously. He had a large soul for a man, containing sundry Queen Anne's men, one with another, like quartetto tables; but it was not a large soul for a poet, and it entertained the universe by potato-patches. He established finally the reign of the literati for the reign of the poets—and the critics clapped their hands. He established finally the despotism of the final emphasis—and no one dared, in affecting criticism, to speak any more at all against a tinkling cymbal. And so in distinctive succession to poetry and inspiration, began the new system of harmony "as by law established;" and so he translated Virgil not only into English but into Dryden; and so he was kind enough to translate Chaucer too, as an example,—made him a much finer speaker, and not according to our doxy, so good a versifier—and cured the readers of the old "Knight's tale" of sundry of their tears; and so he reasoned powerfully in verse—and threw into verse besides, the whole force of his strong sensual being; and so he wrote what has been called from generation to generation, down to the threshold of our days, "the best ode in the English language." To complete which successes, he thrust out nature with a fork; and for a long time, and in spite of Horace's prophecy, she never came back again. Do we deny our gratitude and his glory to glorious John because we speak thus? In nowise would we do it. He was a man greatly endowed; and our language and our literature remain, in certain respects, the greater for his greatness—more practical, more rapid, and with an air of mixed freedom and adroitness which we welcome as an addition to the various powers of either. With regard to his influence—and he was most influential upon POETRY—we have spoken; and have the whole of the opening era from which to prove.

While we return upon our steps for a breathing moment, and pause before Milton,—the consideration occurs to us that a person of historical ignorance in respect to this divine poet, would hesitate and be at a loss to which era of our poetry to attach him through the internal evidence of his works. He has not the tread of a contemporary of Dryden; and Rochester's nothingness is a strange accompaniment to the voice of his greatness. Neither can it be quite predicated of him that he walks an Elizabethan man; there is a certain fine bloom or farina, rather felt than seen, upon the old poems, unrecognized upon his. But the love of his genius leant backward to those olden oracles; and it is pleasant to think that he was actually born before Shakespeare's death; that they too looked upwardly to the same daylight and stars; and that he might have stretched his baby arms ("animosus infans") to the faint hazel eyes of the poet of poets. Let us think in anywise that he drew in some living subtle Shakespearian benediction, providing for greatness.

The Italian poets had "rained influence" on the Elizabethan "field of the cloth of gold;" and from the Italian poets as well as the classical sources and the elder English ones, did Milton accomplish his soul. Yet the poet Milton was not made by what he received; not even by what he loved. High above the current of poetical influences he held his own grand personality; and there never lived poet in any age (unless we assume ignorantly of Homer) more isolated in the contemporaneous world than he. He was not worked upon from out of it, nor did he work outwardly upon it. As Cromwell's secretary and Salmasius's antagonist, he had indeed an audience; but as a poet, a scant one; his music, like the spherical tune, being inaudible because too fine and high. It is almost awful to think of him issuing from the arena of controversy victorious and *blind*,—putting away from his dark brows the bloody laurel, left alone after the heat of the day by those for whom he had combated; and originating in that enforced dark quietude his epic vision for the inward sight of the unborn; so to avenge himself on the world's neglect by exacting from it an eternal future of reminiscence. The circumstances of the production of his great work are worthy in majesty of the poem itself; and the writer is the ideal to us of the majestic personality of a poet. He is the student, the deep thinker, the patriot, the believer, the thorough brave man,—breathing freely for truth and freedom under the leaden weights of his adversities, never reproaching God for his griefs by his despair, working in the chain, praying without ceasing in the serenity of his sightless eyes; and, because the whole visible universe was swept away from betwixt them and the Creator, contemplating more intently the invisible infinite, and shaping all his thoughts to it in grander proportion. O noble Christian poet! Which is hardest? self-renunciation, and the sackcloth and the cave—or grief-renunciation, and the working on, on, under the stripe? He did what was hardest. He was Agonistes building up, instead of pulling down; and his high religious fortitude gave a character to his works. He stood in the midst of those whom we are forced to consider the corrupt versificators of his day, an iconoclast of their idol rhyme, and protesting practically against the sequestration of pauses. His lyrical poems, move they ever so softly, step loftily, and with something of an epic air.

His sonnets are the first sonnets of a free rhythm—and this although Shakespeare and Spenser were sonnetteers. His "Comus," and "Samson," and "Lycidas,"—how are we to praise them? His epic is the second to Homer's, and the first in sublime effects—a sense as of divine benediction flowing through it from end to end. Not that we compare, for a moment, Milton's genius with Homer's; but that Christianity is in the poem besides Milton. If we hazard a remark which is not admiration, it shall be this—that with all his heights and breadths (which we may measure geometrically if we please from the "Davideis" of Cowley)—with all his rapt devotions and exaltations towards the highest of all, we do miss something (we, at least, who are writing, miss something) of what may be called, but rather metaphysically than theologically, *spirituality*. His spiritual personages are vast enough, but not rarefied enough. They are humanities, enlarged, uplifted, transfigured—but no more. In the most spiritual of his spirits, there is a conscious, obvious, even ponderous, materialism. And hence comes the celestial gunpowder, and hence the clashing with swords, and hence the more continuous evil which we feel better than we describe, the thick atmosphere clouding the heights of the subject. And if anybody should retort, that complaining so we complain of Milton's humanity—we shake our heads. For Shakespeare also was a *man;* and our creed is, that the "Midsummer Night's Dream" displays more of the fairyhood of fairies, than the "Paradise Lost" does of the angelhood of angels. The example may serve the purpose of explaining our objection; both leaving us room for the one remark more—that Ben Jonson and John Milton, the most scholastic of our poets, brought out of their scholarship different gifts to our language; that Jonson brought more Greek, and Milton more Latin: while the influences of the latter and greater poet were at once more slowly and more extensively effectual.

Butler was the contemporary of Milton: we confess a sort of continuous "innocent surprise" in the thought of it, however the craziness of our imagination may be in fault. We have stood by as witnesses while the great poet sanctified the visible earth with the oracle of his blindness; and are startled that a profane voice should be hardy enough to break the echo, and jest in the new consecrated temple. But this is rather a roundheaded than a longheaded way of adverting to poor Butler; who, for all his gross injustice to the purer religionists, in the course of "flattering the vices and daubing the iniquities" of King Charles's court, does scarcely deserve at our hands either to be treated as a poet or punished for being a contemporary of the poet Milton. Butler's business was the business of desecration, the exact reverse of a poet's; and by the admission of all the world his business is well done. His learning is various and extensive, and his fancy communicates to it its mobility. His wit has a gesture of authority, as if it might, if it pleased, be wisdom. His power over language, "tattered and ragged" like Skelton's, is as wonderful as his power over images. And if nobody can commend the design of his "Hudibras," which is the English counterpart of Don Quixote,—a more objectionable servility than an adaptation from a serious composition, in which case that humorous effect would have been increased by the travestie, which is actually injured, and precisely in an inverse ratio, by the burlesque copy of the burlesque,—everybody must admit the force of the execution. When Prior attempted afterwards the same line of composition with his peculiar grace and airiness of diction,—when Swift ground society into jests with a rougher turning of the wheel,—still, then and since, has this Butler stood alone. He is the genius of his class; a natural enemy to poetry under the form of a poet: not a great man, but a powerful man.

We return to the generation of Dryden and to Pope his inheritor—Pope, the perfecter, as we have already taken occasion to call him—who stood in the presence of his father Dryden, before that energetic soul, weary with its long literary work which was not always clean and noble, had uttered its last wisdom or foolishness through the organs of the body. Unfortunately, Pope had his advisers apart from his muses;

and their counsel was "be correct." To be correct, therefore, to be great through correctness, was the end of his ambition, an aspiration scarcely more calculated for the production of noble poems than the philosophy of utilitarianism is for that of lofty virtues. Yet correctness seemed a virtue rare in the land; Dr. Johnson having crowned Lord Roscommon over Shakespeare's head, "the only correct writer before Addison." The same critic predicated of Milton, that he could not cut figures upon cherry-stones. Pope glorified correctness, and dedicated himself to cherry-stones from first to last. A cherry-stone was the apple of his eye.

Now we are not about to take up any popular cry against Pope; he has been overpraised and is underpraised; and in the silence of our poetical experience, ourselves may confess personally to the guiltiness of either extremity. He was not a great poet; he meant to be a correct poet, and he was what he meant to be, according to his construction of the thing meant; there are few among us who fulfil so literally their ambitions. Moreover we will admit to our reader in the confessional, that, however convinced in our innermost opinion of the superiority of Dryden's genius, we have more pleasure in reading Pope than we ever could enjoy or imagine under Pope's master. We incline to believe that Dryden being the greatest poet-power, Pope is the best poet-manual; and that whatever Dryden has done—we do not say conceived, we do not say suggested, but *done*—Pope has done that thing better. For translations, we hold up Pope's Homer against Dryden's Virgil and the world. Both translations are utterly and equally contrary to the antique, both bad with the same sort of excellence; but Pope's faults are Dryden's faults, while Dryden's are not Pope's. We say the like of the poems from Chaucer; we say the like of the philosophic and satirical poems: the art of reasoning in verse is admirably attained by either poet, but practised with more grace and point by the later one. To be sure, there is the "Alexander's Feast" ode, called, until people half believed what they said, the greatest ode in the language! But here is, to make the scales even again, the "Eloisa" with tears on it,—faulty but tender—of a sensibility which glorious John was not born with a heart for. To be sure, it was not necessary that John Dryden should keep a Bolingbroke to think for him: but to be sure again, it is something to be born with a heart, particularly for a poet. We recognize besides in Pope, a delicate fineness of tact, of which the precise contrary is unpleasantly obvious in his great master; Horace Walpole's description of Selwyn, *un bête inspiré*, with a restriction of *bête* to the animal sense, fitting glorious John like his crown. Now there is nothing of this coarseness of the senses about Pope; the little pale Queen Anne's valetudinarian had a nature fine enough to stand erect upon the point of a needle like a schoolman's angel; and whatever he wrote coarsely, he did not write from inward impulse, but from external conventionality, from a bad social Swift-sympathy. For the rest, he carries out his master's principles into most excellent and delicate perfection: he is rich in his degree. And there is, indeed, something charming even to an enemy's ear in this exquisite balancing of sounds and phrases, these "shining rows" of oppositions and appositions, this glorifying of commonplaces by antithetic processes, this catching, in the rebound, of emphasis upon rhyme and rhyme; all, in short, of this Indian jugglery and Indian carving upon—cherry-stones! "and she herself" (that is, poetry)—

> And she herself one fair Antithesis.

When Voltaire threw his "Henriade" into the fire and Hénault rescued it, "Souvenez-vous," said the president to the poet, "that I burnt my lace ruffles for the sake of your epic." It was about as much as the epic was worth. For our own part, we would sacrifice not only our point, but the prosperity of our very fingers, to save, from a similar catastrophe, these works of Pope; and this, although the most perfect and original of all of them, "The Rape of the Lock," had its fortune in a fire-safe. They are the works of a master. A great poet? oh no! A true poet?—perhaps not. Yet a man, be it remembered, of such mixed gracefulness and power, that Lady Mary Wortley deigned to coquet with him, and Dennis shook before him in his shoes.

Nature, as we have observed, had been expelled by a fork, under the hand of Pope's progenitors; and if in him and around him we see no sign of her return, we do not blame Pope for what is, both in spirit and in form, the sin of his school. Still less would we "play at bowles" with Byron, and praise his right use of the right poetry of Art. Our views of Nature and of Art have been sufficiently explained to leave our opinion obvious of the controversy in ques tion, in which, as in a domestic broil, "there were faults on both sides." Let a poet never write the words "tree," "hill," "river," and he may still be true to nature. Most untrue, on the other hand, most narrow, is the poetical sectarianism, and essentially most unpoetical, which stands among the woods and fields announcing with didactic phlegm, "Here only is nature." Nature is where God is. Poetry is where God is. Can you go up or down or around and not find Him? In the loudest hum of your machinery, in the dunnest volume of your steam, in the foulest street of your city,—there, as surely as in the Brocken pinewoods, and the watery thunders of Niagara,—there, as surely as He is above all, lie Nature and Poetry in full life. Speak, and they will answer! Nature is a large meaning: let us make room for it in the comprehension of our love!—for the coral rock built up by the insect and the marble column erected by the man.

In this age of England, however, pet-named the Augustan, there was no room either for Nature or Art: Art and Nature (for we will not separate their names) were at least maimed and dejected and sickening day by day—

> Quoth she, I grieve to see your leg
> Stuck in a hole here, like a peg;

and even so, or like the peg of a top humming drowsily, our poetry stood still. There was an abundance of "correct writers," yes, and of "elegant writers:" there was Parnell, for instance, who would be called besides, a pleasing writer by any pleasing critic; and Addison, a proverb for the "virtuousest, discreetest, best" with all the world. Or if, after the Scotch mode of Monkbarns, we call our poets by their possessions, not so wronging their characteristics, there was "The Dispensary," the "Art of Preserving Health," the "Art of Cookery,"—and "Trivia," or the "Fan,"—take Gay by either of those names! and "Cider," or the "Splendid Shilling"—take Phillips, Milton's imitator, by either of these! and there was Pomfret, not our "choice," the concentrate essence of namby-pambyism; and Prior, a brother spirit of the French Gresset,—a half-brother, of an inferior race, yet to be praised by us for one instinct obvious in him, a blind stretching of the hand to a sweeter order of versification than was current. Of Young we could write much: he was the very genius of Antithesis; a genius breaking from "the system," with its broken chain upon his limbs, and frowning darkly through the gray monotony; a grander writer by spasms than by volitions. Blair was of his class, but rougher; a brawny contemplative Orson. And how many of our readers may be unaware of the underground existence of another *Excursion* than the deathless one of our days, and in blank verse, too, and in several cantos; and how nobody will thank us for digging at these fossil remains! It is better to remember Mallet by his touching ballad of the "William and Margaret," a word taken from diviner lips to becoming purpose; only we must not be thrown back upon the "Ballads," lest we wish to live with them forever. Our literature is rich in ballads, a form epitomical of the epic and dramatic, and often vocal when no other music is astir; and to give a particular account of which would take us far across our borders.

As it is, we are across them; we are benighted in our wandering and straitened for room. We glance back vainly to the lights of the later drama, and see Dryden, who had the heart to write rhymed plays after Shakespeare, and but little heart for any thing else,—and Congreve, and Lillo, and Southerne, and Rowe, all gifted writers, and Otway, master of tears, who starved in our streets for his last tragedy—a poet most effective in broad touches; rather moving, as it appears to us, by scenes than by words.

Returning to the general poets, we meet with bent faces toward hill-side Nature, Thomson and Dyer; in writing which names together, we do not depreciate Thomson's how ever we may a little exalt Dyer's. We praise neither of these writers for being descriptive poets; but for that faithful transcript of their own impressions, which is a common subject of praise in both: Dyer being more distinct, perhaps, in his images, and Thomson more impressive in his general effect. Both are faulty in their blank verse diction; the latter too florid and verbose, the former (although "Grongar Hill" is simple almost to baldness) too pedantic and *constructive*—far too "saponaceous" and "pomaceous." We offer pastoral salutation also to Shenstone and Hammond; pairing them like Polyphemus's sheep; fain to be courteous if we could: and we could if we were "Phillida." Surely it is an accomplishment to utter a pretty thought so simply that the world is forced to remember it; and that gift was Shenstone's, and he the most poetical of country gentlemen. May every shrub on the lawn of Leasowes be evergreen to his brow! And next, O most patient reader!—pressed to a conclusion and in a pairing humor, we come to Gray and Akenside together, yes, together! because if Gray had written a philosophic poem he would have written it like the "Pleasures of Imagination," and because Akenside would have written odes like Gray, if he could have commanded a rapture. Gray, studious and sitting in the cold, learnt the secret of a simulated and innocent fire (the Greek fire he might have *called* it), which burns beautifully to the eye, but never would have harmed M. Hénault's ruffles. Collins had twenty times the lyric genius of Gray; we feel his fire in our cheeks. But Gray, but Akenside—both with a volition towards enthusiasm—have an under-constitution of most scholastic coldness: "Si vis me flere," you must weep; but they only take out their pocket-handkerchiefs. We confess humbly, before gods and men, that we never read to the end of Akenside's "Pleasures," albeit we have read Plato: some pleasures, say the moralists, are more trying than pains. Let us turn for refreshment to Goldsmith—that amiable genius, upon whose diadem we feel our hands laid ever and anon in familiar love,—to Goldsmith, half emerged from "the system," his forehead touched with the red ray of the morning; a cordial singer. Even Johnson, the ponderous critic of the system, who would hang a dog if he read "Lycidas" twice, who wrote the lives of the poets and left out the poets, even he loved Goldsmith! and Johnson was Dryden's critical bear, a rough bear, and with points of noble beardom. But while he growled the leaves of the greenwood fell; and oh, how sick to faintness grew the poetry of England! Anna Seward "by'r lady," was the "muse" of those days, and Mr. Hayley "the bard," and Hannah More wrote our dramas, and Helen Williams our odes, and Rosa Matilda our elegiacs,—and Blacklock, blind from his birth, our descriptive poems, and Mr. Whalley our "domestic epics," and Darwin our poetical philosophy, and Lady Millar encouraged literature at Bath, with red taffeta and "the vase." But the immortal are threatened vainly. It was the sickness of renewal rather than of death; St. Leon had his fainting hand on the elixir: the new era was alive in Cowper. We do not speak of him as the master of a transition, only as a hinge on which it slowly turned; only as an earnest tender writer, and true poet enough to be true to himself. Cowper sang in England, and Thomas Warton also, —of a weaker voice but in tune: and Beattie, for whom we have too much love to analyze it, seeing that we drew our childhood's first poetic pleasure from his "Minstrel." And Burns walked in glory on the Scottish mountain's side: and everywhere Dr. Percy's collected ballads were sowing the great hearts of some still living for praise, with impulses of greatness. It was the revival of poetry, the opening of the fifth era, the putting down of the Dryden dynasty, the breaking of the serf bondage, the wrenching of the iron from the soul. And Nature and Poetry did embrace one another! and all men who were lovers of either and of our beloved England, were enabled to resume the pride of their consciousness, and looking round the world say gently, yet gladly, "Our Poets."

When Mr. Wordsworth gave his first poems to the public, it was not well with poetry in England. The "system" riveted upon the motions of poetry by Dryden and his dynasty had gradually added to the restraint of slavery, its weakness and emasculation. The change from poetry to rhetoric had issued in another change, to the commonplaces of rhetoric. We had no longer to complain of Pope's antithetic glories: there was "a vile antithesis" for those also. The followers were not as the master; and the very facility with which the trick of acoustical mechanics was caught up by the former—admitting of "singing for the million," with ten fingers each for natural endowment, and the ability to count them for acquirement,—made wider and more apparent the difference of dignity between the Popes and the Pope Joans. Little by little, by slow and desolate degrees, Thought had perished out of the way of the appointed and most beaten rhythm; and we had the beaten rhythm, without the living footstep—we had the monotony of the military movement, without the heroic impulse—the cross of the Legion of Honor, hung, as it once was, in a paroxysm of converted Bourbonism, at a horse's tail; and the "fork," which expelled nature, dropped feebly downward, blunted of its point. And oh! to see who sat then in England, in the seats of the elders! The Elizabethan men would have gnashed their teeth at such a sight; the Queen Anne's men would have multiplied Dunciads. Of the third George's men (Αχαιΐδες ουκ ετ' Αχαιοι) Hayley, too good a scholar to bear to be so bad a poet, was a chief hope,—and Darwin, mistaker of the optic nerve for the poetical sense, an inventive genius.

But Cowper had a great name, and Burns a greater; and the *réveillé* of Dr. Percy's "Reliques of English Poetry" was echoed presently by the "Scottish Minstrelsy." There was a change, a revival, an awakening, a turning, at least upon the pillow, of some who slept on in mediocrity, as if they felt the daylight on their shut eyelids: there was even a group of noble hearts (Coleridge, the idealist, poet among poets, in their midst), foreseeing the sun. Nature, the long banished, redawned like the morning: Nature, the true mother, cried afar off to her children, "Children, I am here! come to me." It was a hard act to come, and involved the learning and the leaving of much. Conventionalities of phrase and rhythm, conventional dialects set apart for poets, conventional words, attitudes, and manners, consecrated by "wits,"—all such Nessian trappings were to be wrenched off, even to the cuticle into which they had urged their poison. But it was an act not too hard for the doing. There was a visible movement towards nature; the majority moving of course with reservation, but individuals with decision; some rending downward their garments of pestilent embroidery, and casting themselves at her feet. As the chief of the movement, the Xenophon of the return, we are bound to acknowledge this great Wordsworth, and to admire how, in a bravery bravest of all because born of love, in a passionate unreservedness sprung of genius, and to the actual scandal of the world which stared at the filial familiarity, he threw himself not at the feet of Nature, but straightway and right tenderly upon her bosom. And so, trustfully as child before mother, self-renouncingly as child after sin, absorbed away from the consideration of publics and critics as child at play-hours, with a simplicity startling to the *blasé* critical ear as inventiveness, with an innocent utterance felt by the competent thinker to be wisdom, and with a faithfulness to natural impressions acknowledged since by all to be the highest art,—this William Wordsworth did sing his "Lyrical Ballads" where the "Art of criticism" had been sung before, and "the world would not let them die."

The voice of nature has a sweetness which few of us, when sufficiently tried, can gainsay; it penetrates our artificial "tastes," and overcomes us; and our ignorance seldom proves strong, in proportion to our instincts. We recognize, like Ulysses' dog, with feeble joyous gesture the master's voice: and the sound is nearly always pleasant to us, however we may want strength to follow after it. But, while at the period we refer to, the recognition and gratulation were true and deep, the old conventionalities and prejudices hung heavily in bondage and repression. The great body of readers would recoil to the Drydenic rhythm, to the Queen Anne's poetical cant, to anti-Saxonisms whether in Latin or French; or exacted as a condition of a poet's faithfulness to nature, such an effervescence of his emotions, as had rendered Pope natural in the Eloisa. "Let us all forsooth be Eloisa and so natural,"—the want was an excuse for loving nature; and the opinion went, that the daily heart-beat was more obnoxious in poetry, than the incidental palpitation. Poor Byron (true miserable genius, soul-blinded great poet)! ministered to this singular need, identifying poetry and passion. Poetry ought to be the revelation of the complete man—and Byron's manhood having no completion nor entirety, consisting on the contrary of a one-sided passionateness, his poems discovered not a heart, but the wound of a heart; not humanity, but disease; not life, but a crisis. It was not so—

it was not in the projection of a passionate emotion, that William Wordsworth committed himself to nature, but in full resolution and determinate purpose. He is scarcely, perhaps, of a passionate temperament, although still less is he cold; rather quiet in his love, as the stock-dove, and brooding over it as constantly, and with as soft an inward song lapsing outwardly—serene through deepness—saying himself of his thoughts, that they "do often lie too deep for tears;" which does not mean that their painfulness will not suffer them to be wept for, but that their closeness to the supreme Truth hallows them, like the cheek of an archangel, from tears. Call him the very opposite of Byron, who, with narrower sympathies for the crowd, yet stood nearer to the crowd, because everybody understands passion. Byron was a poet through pain. Wordsworth is a feeling man, because he is a thoughtful man; he KNOWS grief itself by a reflex emotion; by sympathy rather than by suffering. He is eminently and humanly expansive; and, spreading his infinite egotism over all the objects of his contemplation, reiterates the love, life, and poetry of his peculiar being in transcribing and chanting the material universe, and so sinks a broad gulf between his descriptive poetry and that of the Darwinian painter-poet school. Darwin was, as we have intimated, all optic nerve. Wordsworth's eye is his soul. He does not see that which he does not intellectually discern, and he beholds his own cloud-capped Helvellyn under the same conditions with which he would contemplate a grand spiritual abstraction. In his view of the exterior world,—as in a human Spinozism,—mountains and men's hearts share in a sublime unity of humanity; yet his Spinozism does in nowise affront God, for he is eminently a religious poet, if not, indeed, altogether as generous and capacious in his Christianity as in his poetry; and being a true Christian poet, he is scarcely least so when he is not writing directly upon the subject of religion; just as we learn sometimes without looking up, and, by the mere color of the grass, that the sky is cloudless. But what is most remarkable in this great writer is, his poetical consistency. There is a wonderful unity in these multiform poems of one man; they are "bound each to each in natural piety," even as his days are: and why? because they *are* his days—all his days, work days and Sabbath days—his life, in fact, and not the unconnected works of his life, as vulgar men do opine of poetry and do rightly opine of vulgar poems, but the sign, seal, and representation of his life—nay, the actual audible breathing of his inward spirit's life. When Milton said that a poet's life should be a poem, he spoke a high moral truth; if he had added a reversion of the saying, that a poet's poetry should be his life,—he would have spoken a critical truth, not low.

"Foole, saide my muse to mee, looke in thine hearte and write,"—and not only, we must repeat, at feast times, fast times, or curfew times—not only at times of crisis and emotion, but at all hours of the clock; for that which God thought good enough to write, or permit the writing of on His book, the heart, is not too common, let us be sure, to write again in the best of our poems. William Wordsworth wrote these common things of nature, and by no means in a phraseology nor in a style. He was daring in his commonness as any of your Tamerlanes may be daring when far fetching an alien image from an outermost world; and, notwithstanding the ribald cry of that "vox populi" which has, in the criticism of poems, so little the character of divinity, and which loudly and mockingly, at his first utterance, denied the sanctity of his simplicities,—the Nature he was faithful to "betrayed not the heart which loved her," but, finally, justifying herself and him, "DID"—without the "Edinburgh Review."

"Hero-worshippers," as we are, and sitting for all the critical pretence—in right or wrong of which we speak at all—at the feet of Mr. Wordsworth,—recognizing him, as we do, as poet-hero of a movement essential to the better being of poetry, as poet-prophet of utterances greater than those who first listened could comprehend, and of influences most vital and expansive—we are yet honest to confess that certain things in the "Lyrical Ballads" which most provoked the ignorant innocent hootings of the mob, do not seem to us all heroic. Love, like ambition, may overvault itself; and Betty Foys of the Lake school (so called) may be as subject to conventionalities as Pope's Lady Bettys. And, perhaps, our great poet might, through the very vehemence and nobleness of his hero and prophet-work for nature, confound, for some blind moment, and, by an association easily traced and excused, nature with rusticity, the simple with the bald; and even fall into a vulgar conventionality in the act of spurning a graceful one. If a trace of such confounding may occasionally be perceived in Mr. Wordsworth's earlier poetry, few critics are mad enough, to-day, to catch at the loose straws of the full golden sheaf and deck out withal their own arrogant fronts, in the course of mouthing mocks at the poet. The veriest critic of straw knoweth well, at this hour of the day, that if Mr. Wordsworth was ever over-rustic, it was not through incapacity to be right royal; that of all poets, indeed, who have been kings in England, not one has swept the purple with more majesty than this poet, when it hath pleased him to be majestic. *Vivat rex*,—and here is a new volume of his reign. Let us rejoice, for the sake of literature and the age, in the popularity which is ready for it, and in the singular happiness of a great poet living long enough to rebound from the "fell swoop" of his poetical destiny, survive the ignorance of his public, and convict the prejudices of his reviewers. It is a literal "poetical justice," and one rarest of all, that a great poet should stand in a permitted sovereignty, without doing so, like poor Inez de Castro, by right of death. It is almost wonderful that his country should clap her hands in praise of him, before he has ceased to hear: the applause resembles an anachronism. Is Mr. Wordsworth startled at receiving from his contemporaries what he expected only from posterity?—is he asking himself, "Have I done any thing wrong?" Probably not: it is at least with his usual air of calm and advised dignity that he addresses his new volume in its *Envoy:*

> Go single,—yet aspiring to be joined
> With thy forerunners, that through many a year,
> Have faithfully prepared each other's way—
> Go forth upon a mission best fulfilled

When and wherever, in this changeful world,
Power hath been given to please for higher ends
Than pleasure only; gladdening to prepare
For wholesome sadness, troubling to refine,
Calming to raise.

—words of the poet, which form a nobler description of the character and uses of his poetry, than could be given in any words of a critic.

We do not say that the finest of Mr. Wordsworth's productions are to be found or should be looked for in the present volume; but the volume is worthy of its forerunners, consistent in noble earnestness and serene philosophy, true poet's work,—the hand trembling not a jot for years or weariness,—the full face of the soul turned hopefully and stilly as ever towards the True, and catching across its ridge the idealized sunlight of the Beautiful. And yet if we were recording angel, instead of only recording reviewer, we should drop a tear—another—and end by weeping out that series of sonnets in favor of capital punishments,—moved that a hand which has traced *life*-warrants so long for the literature of England, should thus sign a misplaced "Benedicite" over the hangman and his victim. We turn away from them to other sonnets—to forget aught in Mr. Wordsworth's poetry we must turn to his poetry:—and however the greatest poets of our country,—the Shakespeares, Spensers, Miltons,—worked upon high sonnet-ground, not one opened over it such broad and pouring sluices of various thought, imagery, and emphatic eloquence as he has done.

The tender Palinodia is beyond Petrarch:—

Though I beheld at first with blank surprise
This work, I now have gazed on it so long,
I see its truth with unreluctant eyes;
O my beloved! I have done thee wrong,
Conscious of blessedness, but, whence it springs
Ever too heedless, as I now perceive:
Morn into noon did pass, noon into eve,
And the old day was welcome as the young,
As welcome and as beautiful—in sooth
More beautiful, as being a thing more holy;
Thanks to thy virtues, to the eternal youth
Of all thy goodness, never melancholy;
To thy large heart and humble mind, that cast
Into one vision, future, present, past!

That "*more beautiful*" is most beautiful: all human love's cunning is in it, besides the full glorifying smile of Christian love.

Last in the volume is the tragedy of "The Borderers," which having lain for some fifty years "unregarded" among its author's papers, —a singular destiny for these printing days when our very morning-talk seems to fall naturally into pica type,—caused, in its announcement from afar, the most faithful disciples to tremble for the possible failure of their master. Perhaps they trembled with cause. The master, indeed, was a prophet of humanity; but he was wiser in love than terror, in admiration than pity, and rather intensely than actively human; capacious to embrace within himself the whole nature of things and beings, but not going out of himself to embrace any thing; a poet of one large sufficient soul, but not polypsychical like a dramatist. Therefore his disciples trembled: and we will not say that the tragedy, taken as a whole, does not justify the fear. There is something grand and Greek in the intention which hinges it, showing how crime makes crime in cursed generation, and how black hearts, like whiter ones (Topaze or Ebène), do cry out and struggle for sympathy and brotherhood; granting that black heart (Oswald) may stand something too much on the extreme of evil to represent humanity broadly enough for a drama to turn upon. The action, too, although it does not, as might have been apprehended, lose itself in contemplation, has no unhesitating firm dramatic march—perhaps it "potters" a little, to take a word from Mrs. Butler;—and when all is done we look vainly within us for an impression, the response to the unity of the whole. But again, when all is done, the work is Mr. Wordsworth's, and the conceptions and utterances living and voiceful in it, bear no rare witness to the master. The old blind man, left to the ordeal of the desert—the daughter in agony hanging upon the murderer for consolation—knock against the heart, and take back answers; and ever and anon there are sweet gushings of such words as this poet only knows, showing how, in a "late remorse of love," he relapses into pastoral dreams, notwithstanding his new vocation, and within the very sight of the theatric *thymele* :—

> A grove of darker and more lofty shade
> I never saw. The music of the birds
> Drops deadened from a roof so thick with leaves.

Who can overpass the image of the old innocent man praying ?—

> The name of daughter on his lips, he prays!
> With nerves so steady, that the very flies
> Sit unmolested on his staff.

But we come hastily to the moral of our story, —seeing that Mr. Wordsworth's life does present a high moral to his generation, to forget which in his poetry would be an unworthy compliment to the latter. It is advantageous for us all, whether poets or poetasters, or talkers about either, to know what a true poet is, what his work is, and what his patience and successes must be, so as to raise the popular idea of these things, and either strengthen or put down the individual aspiration. "Art," it was said long ago, "requires the whole man," and "Nobody," it was said later, "can be a poet who is any thing else;" but the present idea of Art requires the segment of a man, and everybody who is any thing at all, is a poet in a parenthesis. And our shelves groan with little books over which their readers groan less metaphorically; there is a plague of poems in the land apart from poetry; and many poets who live and are true, do not live by their truth, but hold back their full strength from Art because they do not *reverence* it fully; and all booksellers cry aloud and do not spare, that poetry will not sell; and certain critics utter melancholy frenzies, that poetry is worn out forever—as if the morning-star was worn out from heaven, or "the yellow primrose" from the grass; and Mr. D'Israeli the younger, like Bildad comforting Job, suggests that we may content ourselves for the future with a rhythmetic prose, printed like prose for decency, and supplied, for comfort, with a parish allowance of two or three rhymes to a paragraph. Should there be any whom such a "New Poor Law" would content, we are far from wishing to disturb the virtue of their serenity: let them continue, like the hypochondriac, to be very sure that they have lost their souls, inclusive of their poetic instincts. In the mean time the hopeful and believing will hope,—trust on; and, better still, the Tennysons and the Brownings,* and other high-gifted spirits, will work, wait on, until, as Mr. Horne has said—

> Strong deeds awake
> And clamoring, throng the portals of the hour.

It is well for them and all to count the cost of this life of a master in poetry, and learn from it what a true poet's crown is worth; to recall both the long life's work for its sake—the work of observation, of meditation, of reaching past models into nature, of reaching past nature unto God; and the early life's loss for its sake—the loss of the popular cheer, of the critical assent, and of the "money in the purse." It is well and full of exultation to remember *now* what a silent, blameless, heroic life of poetic duty, this

* Any reader who may have neglected to note the closing remark of the preface to this book is reminded that the above allusion was penned before Miss Elizabeth Barrett foresaw that she was to add the name of Browning to her own.—T. T.

man has lived; how he never cried rudely against the world because he was excluded for a time from the parsley garlands of its popularity; nor sinned morally because he was sinned against intellectually; nor, being tempted and threatened by paymaster and reviewer, swerved from the righteousness and high aims of his inexorable genius. And it cannot be ill to conclude by enforcing a high example by some noble precepts which, taken from the "Musophilus" of old Daniel, do contain, to our mind, the very code of chivalry for poets:—

Be it that my unseasonable song
  Come out of Time, that fault is in the Time;
And I must not do virtue so much wrong
  As love her aught the worse for other's crime.

. . . . . .

And for my part, if only one allow
  The care my laboring spirits take in this,
He is to me a theatre large enow,
  And his applause only sufficient is—
All my respect is bent but to his brow;
  That is my all, and all I am is his.

And if some worthy spirits be pleased too,
  It shall more comfort breed, but not more will,
BUT WHAT IF NONE? *It cannot yet undo*
  The love I bear unto this holy skill:
This is the thing that I was born to do,
  This is my scene, this part must I fulfil.

THE END.

www.ingramcontent.com/pod-product-compliance
Lightning Source LLC
LaVergne TN
LVHW050525100826
845148LV00002B/447

* 9 7 8 1 4 2 5 5 2 0 2 9 8 *